# Beyond the Map

## 5000 Miles of Faith - Robertson to Mocuba and Back

# Beyond the Map

## 5000 Miles of Faith - Robertson to Mocuba and Back

Pink and purple

Reverend Rosalie Weller
B.Ed(Hons), Lic.Theol., B.Soc.Sci(Hons)

Copyright© Reverend Rosalie Weller 2026

All rights reserved

No part of this book may be reproduced, or stored in a retrieval system, or transmitted in any form or by any means, electronic, mechanical, photocopying, recording or otherwise, without express written permission of the publisher. Requests should be made to rosalieweller70@gmail.com

The right of Reverend Rosalie Weller to be identified as the author of this book has been asserted.

Scripture quotations taken from the Holy Bible, New International Version ®NIV® copyright © 1973 1978 2011 by Biblica Inc. Tm used by permission

ISBN: 9798243971843

**Dedication**

To our descendants so that they may know more of us than just a line in a census form.

## CONTENTS

1. Out of our Comfort Zone ................. 7
2. Blowing Away the Grey Cloud ................. 21
3. The Best Laid Plans and Elephant Dung ................. 31
4. Great Wall Motors ................. 45
5. Cross Words ................. 57
6. God's Solutions ................. 65
7. The Kruger National Park ................. 71
8. Border Crossing ................. 79
9. Palm Sunday 2017 ................. 89
10. Mocuba at Last ................. 97
11. The Missionaries ................. 105
12. Easter Weekend ................. 115
13. Mozambique ................. 127
14. Dreams and Epiphanies ................. 135

15. Back in South Africa.................................................143

16. Missions Impossible Completed.............................147

About the Author ...........................................................154

# Foreward

As a child, I sang in Sunday school, 'Every day with Jesus is sweeter than the day before.' This book – a journal, a testimony and a searingly honest reflection, all in one – reminds me that the words of that chorus might not be entirely accurate, however devout one's faith. Rosalie Weller has produced a missionary account that would be useful reading for anyone contemplating overseas service in a culture alien to their own. The hardships are laid bare. The fear and trauma are sometimes almost tangible within the pages. Yet, crucially, so too is Rosalie's trust in God, which underpins every experience and each painful learning curve. The call of the Lord Jesus upon one's life does not come with any promises at all of ease along the way, but only steadfast reassurances of his abiding presence at every step. Rosalie and Syd have lived out those promises, and their story is all the richer for having done so. Hallelujah!

Stephen Poxon
Editor, "Christian Writer", magazine of the Association of Christian Writers,
Author, "With Dickens at Christmas", "Poolies at heart: Celebrating Hartlepool United's Finest"

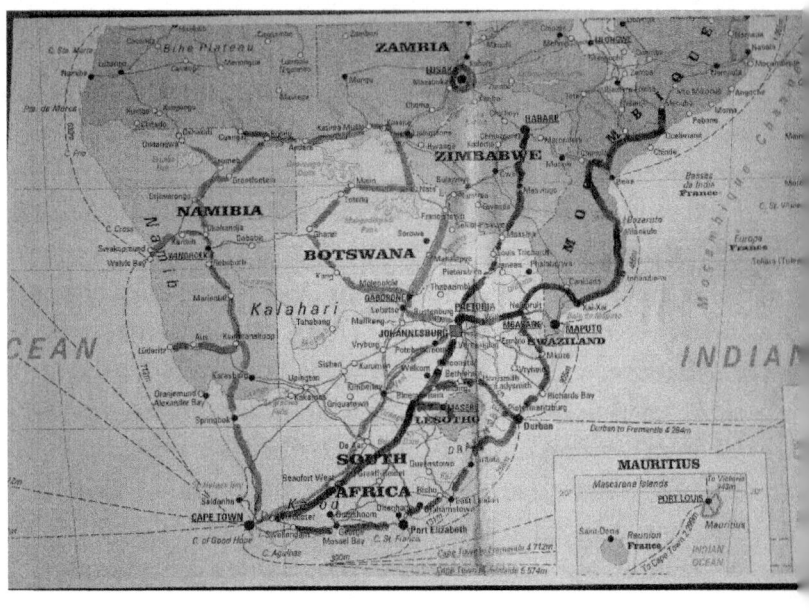

# 1. Out of our Comfort Zone

I burst into tears. It was just another bump in the road, but I couldn't hold it together any longer. My body was shuddering to the tune of the truck; the emotional state triggered a persistent pain radiating upward into my spine and downward into my buttocks and down my right leg, with an excruciating ache of the coccyx, a frequent visitor. An unusual inner fragility caught me unawares as fear supplanted faith. We had been driving for five days and nights without much rest and no stretching of the legs. I was used to travelling, and in this truck, but this was different from any other journey we had accomplished. Two hours of driving on roads where the potholes were as wide as a quarter of the road and as deep as a half of the tyre was too much for me. Beads of sweat began to form in my palms. I started to panic. How long would the road be like this? The knowledge that we would have to return on this same road occurred to me. How could I endure such torture?

The truck shuddered to the right as the front wheels entered the crater. My body swerved, then jarred uncomfortably. We were on the national road from Inchope to Caia in northern Mozambique. It was 2017. I was with my husband of over forty years. He was seventy years old, and I was three and a half years younger. I couldn't blame him. Neither of us could have known just how bad these Mozambican roads would be.

I blamed myself. How had I allowed myself to be in this situation again? Miles from safety and comfort, no mobile phone signal, no map, unable to speak the language and a real possibility that the vehicle I was in would break down. The words of Oliver Hardy, the slapstick comedian of the 1920s, came into my head.

"That's another fine mess you've got us into!" I spoke the words aloud. Syd laughed, and so did I. It had broken the tension. My crying was the unexpected response to our situation. It just wasn't like me. My usual response was sufferance, not anger, not swearing, but putting up with it. We laughed at the situation, and at our ignorance of the place we were in.

Syd's vulnerability only came to the fore at moments like these. He was amazingly strong, both physically and emotionally. He was the man you wanted around when dirt hit the fan but the one thing he couldn't handle was when I was upset and he couldn't solve the immediate problem.

But just how did we get here? This is what this book is about. How do two British pensioners take off their carpet slippers and travel so far from home? What passion guided us? It is also about the mysterious God whom we serve through Jesus Christ. He has protected, provided and privileged us to be partners in His great scheme of things. But it is more than that. It is an exploration of what missionaries are and do. What does it mean to be a missionary? Why do we Christians admire and revere them? Are they the superheroes of Christianity?

> There's a grand highway which is free to all.
> And it leads to the King above.
> It starts at the cross where Jesus died.
> It is there you must join the road.
> Tramp! Tramp! Tramp! I hear them marching. Hark! Hark! Hark!
> The pilgrims sing.
> And that highway will be my way.
> I am going to see the King.

My husband, Syd, had travelled extensively, firstly with the Royal Navy, then with the South Africans. He was fearless, could negotiate different cultures, and enjoyed visiting unknown places. You could say 'off the beaten track' was his forte. I was totally unlike him.

In 2015, retired in England, Syd suggested that we revisit the Kruger National Park, when we went to see our daughter, Maria, who was living in South Africa. Comparable to the size of the country of Wales, covering two million hectares, Kruger's natural habitats are a photographer's paradise. Rounding a bend, you might encounter foraging giraffes and elephants or be thrilled to catch a glimpse of wild dogs around a recent kill, as I did in 2014. I beamed. Did I want to go to the Kruger Park? You bet. In 2016, as we were planning our trip and as the idea of another long journey in the truck began to settle with me, Syd made another suggestion.

"Maybe we could go through the northern gate and into Mozambique."

I was uncertain. We had travelled through the Kruger entering and exiting several of the 11 gates but never out of South Africa. The plan had changed since I had agreed to go. My elder sister, who was living in Johannesburg had told me about her visit to Maputo the previous year. Her words reverberated in my head.

"Frequent power cuts, grimy accommodation, endless hours of driving to nowhere, oppressive heat."

The hook of yet another long road trip through Africa had been the Kruger Park, but now the vision had changed, and danger had entered the mix. Our previous African trips had been to English-speaking countries, which were well travelled by South Africans. Portuguese-speaking Northern Mozambique was not in that league.

Maria lived in Robertson, east of Cape Town. We always visited her first before venturing to another country. That meant almost certainly three days' driving before you encountered virgin soil. Cape Town is on the southern tip of Africa. Exploring other African countries meant you had to travel north. Syd had a thirst for driving to different countries. It probably originated from his days in the South African Navy when he frequently drove the 927 miles from Simon's Town to Pretoria in one day.

I felt trapped. In prayer I asked God what do I do next? I didn't want to disappoint Syd by refusing to travel into Mozambique after we'd done what I wanted, photographing the animals in the Kruger Park. Yet that fear of the unknown, of being on the edge of uncertainty came at me. Is marriage always a trade-off? You give up something in return for gaining something you want.

Mozambique. Why Mozambique? Was there more ruminating in Syd's head than what he had revealed? We knew a couple, Eugene and Tina from the Presbyterian church in Fish Hoek, who had become missionaries in Mozambique. But we hadn't seen them for years. We occasionally contributed to their mission work and received a newsletter but that was all low-key. Was this suggestion something to do with visiting them? We had been robbed of a chance to go to South America as missionaries. Was there a connection? Sometimes these questions are better unspoken, left to surface until the allotted time; a bit like an unset jelly waiting to go into the fridge.

You will have realised that I am a committed Christian. I accept it is not a lifestyle that many choose but I did. I made the choice 40 years ago when I was 27 years old, divorced and with a daughter. Up until that point I had been an atheist – a position many will identify with.

*One night, in the early hours while dreaming, I heard a voice. It was not audible to the human ear as another voice would be. It was inside me. It said,*

*"Jesus Christ has washed away your sins."*

*Peace enveloped me. Joy beyond happiness, beyond birthday presents, incomparable to the stirrings of first love, but it was there. Flooding in besides it, were hundreds of Bible verses faithfully learnt as a child, at Sunday school. It seems impossible but it is true. I cannot explain it. From then I just knew there was a God.*

As it happened during our yearly Maria visit, in February 2016, Syd and Mike, our son, visited Addo Elephant Park in Port Elizabeth once again riding in our bakkie (truck). The temperature that year was the highest it had ever been. It reached 50 degrees centigrade; with the result that Syd had a problem with his undercarriage. This led to a consultation with the local doctor. No treatment was required with the present problem, but the internal examination had revealed a hardness of the prostate. The doctor insisted that a biopsy was necessary as a precaution. The biopsy was not without problems. The next day revealed that Syd had an infection, triggered during the surgery. His return to normal life was delayed as the doctors struggled to name this blight. The troublemaker was e-coli. A further two days in hospital delayed our Kruger/Mozambique trip. It didn't dampen Syd's enthusiasm to travel. I felt that if he wanted to travel, his naval healthcare was covered within the boundaries of South Africa, but I was worried about what would happen if we went outside the borders. At the last minute, after intense discussion, we changed our trip from Kruger and Mozambique to Kruger and Swaziland. Swaziland was still within the boundaries of South Africa.

*I phoned Maria and told her of her dad's condition, shivering, delirious, unable to get up. I was scared. I knew I couldn't drive to Worcester. I didn't have the confidence to go those 50 kilometres on unfamiliar terrain.*

"I'll be over in five minutes," Maria said, "He only came out of hospital yesterday, what's going on?"

"The doctor warned me to go back if I don't feel any improvement. He told me, people die from this." Syd said.

"Come on," Maria commanded, "I'm taking you back in immediately."

*I went too, feeling a total failure because I couldn't drive him. He was very ill. He had to stay in hospital and received intravenous antibiotics and couldn't leave until a tablet version of the medication could be found.*

It may seem that I am glossing over major incidents in our lives without detail or thought. With God in my life, these moments were happening so frequently, and this story is partly about how God provided for me and protected me on just one of our memorable trips through Africa, to Mozambique. This story is mine but includes my husband, but he has his own tale to tell which understandably will be from his angle and must still be written.

I retired in 2011, and Syd did the same in 2013. By 2016, we were enjoying a dual life. We lived most of the year in England but as our daughter was still living in South Africa when we returned to England as missionaries in 2001, we enjoyed an extended holiday time with her in the English winter. We spent anything from six to ten weeks in South Africa.

To make the most of the time in South Africa and to use our money wisely in the long term, we had bought a house in Robertson while we were working in the UK, as well as a newish bakkie from our son-in-law.

The South African bakkie was a wonder to behold - a pickup truck used in the construction industry. They usually ran on economic diesel fuel, were not particularly comfortable but very practical. The length, at about seven feet, meant that they were great to sleep in if you were several inches under six feet as well. In the working day they were used to transport large pieces of timber, and other construction materials. The pleasant weather meant you didn't need a cover. You saw them everywhere in South Africa.

Our bakkie had a removable canopy which was great for its dual function. Sandor, our son-in-law, had bought a bespoke mattress to go in the back, cut out around the wheel arches. I had sewn curtains and fixed them by using wires, hooks and eyes. Completed with duvet and pillows, it was comfortable. Syd fitted a 12v extension to the cabin and we entertained ourselves at night with a portable DVD player and lots of box sets of programmes we loved. We cooked on portable Calor Gas rings and available braaipleke (BBQ places).

Our house in South Africa would have been a retirement house, if that had been God's plan. It was a big house with a garage which Syd had transformed into our living accommodation. The rent from the main house and a small Navy pension covered all our needs in South Africa, so we didn't need to exchange any English money during our winter stay.

Although Syd was still recovering from the illness, he was determined, we would take time out in Africa before we returned to England. In 2016, our trip was to Swaziland and not to Mozambique. For Syd, this was a compromise, but I had managed to persuade him that travelling outside South Africa, where he did not have Naval Medical would be too risky for him and would only exacerbate my anxiety level.

A trip through the Kruger Park was possible again. Sighting a leopard in a baobab tree was exhilarating. The resultant photograph was stunning. I hung it proudly on my English bedroom wall, along with other memorable African photographs taken by me. There's something deeply satisfying about hanging a photo up which you have taken yourself. Your invested energy and patience stand proudly for all to witness and for you to remember.

For the trip north we used a different route than our previous trips, taking the N2 travelling up the east coast of South Africa. We passed through the Transkei, home of Nelson Mandela and noted the small hills of fertile grassland, subdivided into small plots so subsistence farmers could make a meagre living. Much of the land seemed to be uncultivated.

Our overnight stop was at Kokstad at the Nolangeni Hotel, where the staff were gracious enough to provide a delicious meal for latecomers. The border crossing into Swaziland was simple, with only passport stamping needed. The roads were well maintained and empty, very few vehicles travelling. Bordering these wide highways were fields and fields of sugarcane enjoying the sunshine. An eerie rustling of the plants standing well over fifteen feet reminded me of the story of the triffids. I was glad when we pulled into a campsite.

The campsite was basic, with large plots marked out, but at a central hall you could buy drinks and some food. There was also a cultural village to gain some insight into the traditions of the Swazi people. Traditional thatched domes stood proudly with a wooden door barely three feet high. Inside it was very dark and gloomy but cool. There were different huts for sleeping and cooking.

After pitching our tent, we drove out to see the official royal residence. The road leading to the palace was empty of traffic and lined with palm trees. Stray cows chewed at the vegetation on the central divide. There was an abandoned feel to the area like a ghost town. The residence was not open to the public, but its opulence was obvious as we drove around it. These snapshots were part of a rich cultural heritage on offer, although it was more like a drive-through rather than a sit-down meal. Yet we were able to put Mozambique on the back burner, as we ticked off a visit to another country - Swaziland.

*A cyclist pedalled into the camp late afternoon. He carried the minimum of gear, a lightweight small tent. One cycle amongst many trucks, SUVs, camper vans and caravans. Where was he going? Where had he come from?*

*"Hi," said Syd, "You believe in travelling light".*

*"I'm from Poland. I've cycled through Africa over 22,200 kilometres. I am going now to Johannesburg to catch my flight back to Poland."*

*He was a man of few words. His weather-beaten ruddy face belied his many travels. He was finishing the last part of his amazing journey but didn't revel in the glory of it.*

*We saw him the following morning, wheeling his bike with its broken chain and offered him a lift, which he declined.*

*"I either walk or cycle. In the next village is someone who can help me repair the bike. I must do this by myself," he said.*

Why did this cyclist endure such tough conditions to achieve his goal and not take an easier mode of transport? What was the point? Some explorers reported when asked why they did what they achieved, said "because it was there", or "because I could". Meeting this man caused me to ponder on why Syd was so driven in exploring different countries in Africa.

We continued to the Kruger Park visiting several rest camps, Berg-en-Dal, Satara and Skukuza. I did manage to get some great photographs. That trip was full of joy, attending two weddings, travelling to both Kruger and Addo Elephant Park, progressing the conversion of the garage in our house and just enjoying the company of friends and especially Maria and Sandor.

The biopsy which Syd had, revealed prostate cancer in an early stage. He was given a Gleason score of 7. It was God's grace that a minor problem led to investigations which would have otherwise remained hidden and malignant. The consultant was certain. Surgery within six months was essential. Although shocked by the diagnosis, Syd decided to wait and have further tests in England when we returned. Yes, it was a great trip apart from the added burden we carried home with us.

On 15 March, after an almost three-month stay in Africa we returned to England. Syd's doctor's appointment, which we had pushed to the background, shuffled into the foreground. What would the English doctors say? Would they agree that immediate surgery was necessary?

## 2. Blowing Away the Grey Cloud

As we returned to England, it could have been 2001 again, and not 2016. Everything seemed so strange. The hustle and bustle of English life soon replaced the laid-back intimacy of South Africa. We swapped hot, balmy days for cloudy, overcast skies. Culture shock hit me. Our grandchildren had grown, and they were overwhelmed to see us again. Over ten weeks is a long time for children under ten.

Our return to the UK in 2001 had been purpose-driven and a compromise. We had been accepted for service for the Council for World Mission and were waiting to go to British Guiana on the edge of the Amazon Forest. Syd was eager, imagining all the practical help he could give to our mission. I had specialised in cross-cultural ministry in Fish Hoek while developing a project in a mixed-race township. This was a perfect fit for the missionary work in British Guiana.

We sold our house and prepped our eighteen-year-old son who would come with us and the other members of the family. Our house and furniture had been sold, and we had resigned from our jobs. We were waiting to receive the final email with our flight details. The email arrived but related that the funding had been withdrawn, and we could no longer be sent there.

"Lord Jesus, help us; what do we do now?"

A few days later, CWM informed us that they had another post we could take, in England. The dream of the Amazon Forest had dissipated into a grey-clouded Cotswold sky. God had called us in 1982 and sent us to South Africa from England. So, in 2001 we were sent to Gloucestershire to two depleted churches of the Congregational Federation, as missionary partners and pastors.

Our return to England in March 2016 presented us with quite a different problem on our minds. *The image in my head was of sitting by the bed with Syd in the Worcester Hospital, South Africa, where he had had the biopsy and the GP whom he had first seen, entering the room with a grim face. I didn't know whether it would be good or bad news. The South African protocols are so different from the UK. As the doctor said the word cancer, I reached out for Syd's hand. I didn't need to say anything. He knew I was standing with him through this next part of our lives.*

Both situations, in 2001 and in 2016 reminded me that God's ways can be baffling. Both Syd and I wanted to do mission work in British Guiana. My previous experience of setting up a church in a township uniquely qualified me for a cross-cultural ministry. It was puzzling. Why didn't we go? We had prayed. We'd talked it through with each other and with the mission organisation. Everything was set. Then it fell through. Neither of us understood why.

Acknowledging this helped me to accept some of the unexpected things in our lives. We didn't discuss this bombshell with the family. Syd said he wanted to keep it to ourselves, for the time being. Maria in South Africa was the only one who knew as she had been waiting outside and said as soon as she saw the local doctor enter the hospital room, she knew it was bad news. That was the modus operandi of the doctor whom she knew personally through her hospice work. She was sworn to secrecy.

The family saw us as a retired couple enjoying our lives and taking opportunities to visit locations in Europe, without a care in the world. We visited Snowdonia, Minehead for the Spring Harvest Conference, York, Leiston, Norfolk. We also had plenty of time to spend with the family that year.

The NHS served us well. After a doctor's appointment, Syd was quickly referred to the consultant with his South African diagnosis. The consultant recommended a template biopsy which took more cores from the prostate, which would yield a more accurate picture. This was an overnight stay, and the NHS diagnosis was encouraging. The Gleason score was downgraded from 7 to 6. Syd's PSA was within acceptable parameters, a very low score of 3.6. An MRI revealed that the cancer had not spread to other organs. No, immediate surgery would not be recommended. Once again God had blindsided us. What was He doing?

Contrary to what you would expect, Syd and I were flummoxed. How could two consultations be so different?

Surgery or "Watch and Wait"? Returning to South Africa for surgery would also have presented practical problems, if Syd should take that option. Syd decided to watch and wait. Rather nervously we continued on this course for the rest of 2016. Syd went for his appointments, and we didn't share the information with anybody.

We enjoyed several caravan holidays around the UK during that summer. In October Syd celebrated his seventieth birthday. Maria came to celebrate with us, as did many of Syd's family from London. Unbeknown to anyone else, Syd had a special reason and was exceptionally pleased to celebrate, giving God the glory for seventy precious years. I too gave God thanks for him but always the grey cloud of cancer hovered over us.

The Internet provided so much information on all sorts of diseases and options of treatments. We discovered Proton therapy was another treatment carried out by hospitals in Prague. Conveniently, heavily discounted city breaks afforded a trip to Prague. Noone knew a hospital was on our itinerary. Our hopes were raised as we read the information about this new treatment on the website. Could this be the right treatment for Syd?

We travelled to Prague on the weekend of 26-28 February 2017. Although difficult to get to without a car, we arrived to find a state-of-the-art modern hospital. We took a place in the queue, but the first interview revealed one vital piece of information which had not appeared on the website. You could not be considered for Proton treatment if you have had a hip replacement. Syd had his right hip replaced in 2012.

There is something unnerving about just waiting when you have a cancer diagnosis. It seemed that something should be done, an operation or removal of the cancer. At that time, we also heard bad news that one of our South African neighbours, had recently died from prostate cancer after receiving brachytherapy. There seemed to be many individuals with different outcomes suffering from this disease.

About this time, another friend from church received the same diagnosis but with a PSA of 160. He received hormone treatment and some radiotherapy but died within two years of diagnosis. The treatment of 'watch and wait' is more harrowing than immediate treatment being given. Suddenly we became aware of prostate cancer being everywhere. There was also a national awareness campaign started and information about this type of cancer was in your face, everywhere. As we watched and waited, we got on with our lives.

Then we received a newsletter from our friends Eugene and Tina Wessels. They had been serving the Lord as missionaries in Mozambique for eighteen years. He held several retreats for pastors in his area during the year and was organising his annual Bible study training for new pastors in Mocuba. Describing the growth of the missions, he mentioned that their lack of visitors was because they were so far north in the country. In a personal email to Syd, he invited us to help him with his Bible teaching week. He remarked again that in the years he and Tina had been in Mozambique, they had had very few visitors to see their work. Within the spaces of his letter, Syd discerned the need for encouragement from outsiders.

"Where's Mocuba," I asked.

"Mozambique," Syd replied.

Silence but not stillness hung in the air. My mind was in turmoil, oh Lord, I didn't want to go to Mozambique. But I would like to help Eugene with the Bible teaching. Another trade off. It would somehow make another dangerous journey in Africa worthwhile.

"Rosalie, what do think? We could do the same as last year. Kruger, then Mocuba here we come. Eugene has sent all the directions and all the things we need to know in a further email."

"Hmm," I replied.

Syd's health had not deteriorated. He was still on the NHS 'Watch and Wait' programme. His PSA levels were monitored every six months. We had medical cover in South Africa, so we began to plan our next trip. A provisional date was set, leaving England on 18 March and to include a trip to Mozambique.

I printed Eugene's instructions and read them through. One paragraph caught my eye,

"From Rio Save to Muxunge, Gorongozo and Inchope there are a couple of places where the road is pretty good, but be careful, because essentially bad road is with you now for the remainder of the trip."

I read those words but did not ingest them. I was not the driver. On all our trips I made it clear to Syd, I'll go with you, but I don't want to do any driving. He respected that. The full depravity of the road did not sink in. I was swept away by the promise of excellent photo opportunities. We hadn't seen Eugene and Tina for twenty years. They had moved to Mozambique to be missionaries – an idea we had toyed with, but it had been snatched from our grasp. It would be great to see them again and maybe contribute to their worthy cause. After all, I had spent four years in academic education and ten years of practical experience in the ministry to become ordained in the Uniting Presbyterian Church of Southern Africa. Might as well put it to good use. I had been told by CWM that I was the only one to have completed all twelve of their missionary units in my preparation time. Was that pride creeping in?

Aware that the variety and availability of goods are more limited in South Africa, I used the remaining few weeks to gather as much information as I could. Useful telephone numbers, information about roaming technology on my android smart phone, and information on

Mozambique, and I packed my laptop with the Bible studies on it. How would we cope? We didn't speak Portuguese.

Eugene helpfully said he would interpret, as I shared teaching on the Prison Letters of Paul. Also, he would translate my power point if I forwarded it to him. How would that work out? I'd never worked with an interpreter.

For Syd, the grey cloud of cancer had been blown away temporarily by the excitement of visiting another African country. I didn't have the heartlessness to dampen his enthusiasm, but the tsunami of fear had just appeared on the horizon. I had felt that knotting in the stomach and the irrational tide of rising pressure before, in August 1982.

*The baby conceived in England but to be born in South Africa was two weeks late. Pains in the abdomen assailed me and I asked Syd to take me to the military hospital, an hour away. The pains could not be called contractions. They wouldn't bow to human timing. I groaned and sighed the whole journey.*

*On entry, the hospital staff put me on medication to induce the birth and called a gynaecologist. Hours ticked by. Syd felt my damp head and watched my pale body failing. He demanded something be done. A nurse wheeled in a machine to monitor the baby's heartbeat, and a young doctor appeared. I heard a whisper,*

*"There is no heartbeat. The baby is dead. We can't reach the surgeon but if something is not done quickly, your wife will also be dead."*

*I prayed to Jesus, not understanding what was happening. I had heard that whisper. Now I would find out if what I believed was true. Was there a heaven? Was Jesus waiting for me? I was curious rather than concerned. I thought of Daniel entering the Lions' den. He had said, if God wants to, He can save me and if He doesn't, I will still serve Him. That was how I felt.*

*It was Syd's faith, cooperating with the Holy Spirit, which saved the day. The surgeon did not turn up and Syd gave the ordinary doctor permission to perform an emergency caesarean section.*

*He challenged God, "Why did you bring me to this country for my wife and child to die? I do not accept this. Do something."*

*He said at that moment he knew by faith that God had answered his prayer. Our son, our fifth child, was pulled out of a pool of blood and put in an incubator, alive. The placenta had ruptured and starved baby Sam of oxygen. The internal bleeding was causing my death.*

The thought of driving through a wild African country made my heart beat faster but the Lord Jesus would be with me. Besides it would be interesting to see an example of genuine missionary endeavours. What currency do they use in Mozambique? American dollars? Another detail to investigate.

# 3. The Best Laid Plans and Elephant Dung

"Syd," I asked, "Does our African guidebook have a section on Mozambique?"

Syd knew my obsession with planning. "I don't know," he replied. "Anyway, that book is in South Africa. We won't need it. We just go through the northeast gate in Kruger and join up with the national highway in Mozambique and keep going. Don't go buying any more books. We don't want to spend money unnecessarily, do we?"

Syd was being sensible and logical. I wasn't totally convinced and Amazon supplied me with an adequate Portuguese phrasebook, just in case. I was tempted to buy a map of Mozambique, but I resisted. My planning had started. Our tickets to South Africa were booked for 18 March, an overnight flight, arriving on the 19th. We were not novices at trekking across Africa. We had lived near Cape Town for many years. Syd had eighteen years' experience in the South African Defence Force, and our return holiday invariably included an exploration further afield.

In 2013, we had driven over 6000 kilometres from Robertson to Botswana and Zambia. Going eastwards, we had crossed the Caprivi Strip and headed southwards through Namibia, stopping off at the Etosha Pan, the Namibian National Park. We managed and enjoyed the trip, even though we forgot to take our spare tyre. 6000 kilometres without a spare tyre, and by God's grace, we didn't get a puncture!

Etosha was the highlight of that trip for me. Although similar to Kruger in that it is a national park, we saw huge herds of animals, rather than small groups, living in their natural habitat, zebras, elephants, antelope in an awesome salt pan environment. A panorama of nature, a dusty whiteness, presented itself for admiration.

So, what planning did we have to do? Firstly, we had to liaise with Maria and Sandor for the overall ten weeks we would be out of the UK. Eugene's Bible week was already set as Monday 10 April until Friday the 14$^{th}$. As usual, for this Mozambique trip, I took on the role of logistics officer, Syd was the driver. I checked the weather in Mozambique in April. It was going to be very hot more than 40 degrees centigrade. Fuel was about half the price as in South Africa. I worked out how much money we would need for the trip. We were funding it ourselves. Yes, we could afford it, using campsites and bed and breakfast rather than expensive hotels.

This trip would be no different from the previous ones to Zambia and Namibia – hours of arduous driving spiced with sightings of wild animals and made palatable with occasional stimulating conversation. Syd liked to chat while driving and usually there were one or two humourous quips to laugh at. Doing crosswords was my thing. Yes, this trip would be the same as usual, or so I thought.

As the driver, Syd took responsibility for the bakkie. Driving your own vehicle was not only cheaper than public transport but it gave a freedom which you didn't have when travelling in a group or on a guided tour. We took a tent and cooking facilities, as well as our clothes, which were carried inside as we drove. When we reached a campsite, we emptied all our goods into the tent and slept in the back of the bakkie.

One thing I always hated was that Syd sprayed 'Doom' in the bed of the truck and set a mosquito net over the whole truck to keep out the goolies. The insect spray was overpowering, and the netting was claustrophobic. I remonstrated about that but usually I lost out to Syd's logic about the necessity.

The South African weather was made for these trips. The BBQ and Calor Gas two-ring burner made excellent cooking facilities. Add the kettle and it was a worthwhile trip. Half a dozen tins of food sat next to the emergency first aid kit. A cool box powered by the car battery held cold drinks and milk. I insisted on an adequate supply of bottled water after hearing horrendous tales of people dying from thirst after their vehicles broke down in desert areas. That was an argument I won. Most campsites we had been to in South Africa had excellent ablution blocks. Hot showers and hairdryers were readily available. As you might have deduced, this was minimalist camping, with no frills.

For entertainment, we had renewed our collection of DVDs. When we grew tired of listening to the low, slow rumble of lions confirming their territories, we had an alternative. Most interesting was the swapped information and chatting to fellow travellers in the campsites in South Africa.

On 18 March 2017, we left Heathrow for Cape Town – an 11-hour flight. I was excited. We would see our daughter for a couple of weeks before we went on our travels. For Maria, this was a promise kept. Syd had given her his word when we left South Africa in 2001, he would make sure I returned every year to spend some time with her. He kept his promise.

Maria had gone to South Africa with our blended family as a child of ten. Her four siblings had all returned to England when they turned eighteen. She loved Africa, married a South African and looked forward to our visits. Unable to have children, she carved out a career in hospice management, serving on the National Hospice Committee and visiting Kenya and Wisconsin to deliver academic papers at various conferences. Hospice was still in the early stages of development in South Africa and developed care as home-based with many nurses walking and cycling to their patch and few hospital beds. Originally dealing with cancer, this movement came to the forefront in the care of HIV/Aids patients.

I was close to Maria. You may have guessed she was my biological child. We always spent time together during our trips, just doing ordinary things like shopping, going to the cinema and eating out. We booked into various workshops over the years. This year it was cake decorating in Cape Town. Previously we had attended a pottery workshop, and making coffee like a barista. One year she had hijacked me to do a workshop at a national hospice conference about different death rituals in various cultures.

We shared a love of photography, both owning Canon cameras with powerful zoom lenses for wildlife shots. We enjoyed reading and swapped books. Ally McBeal and The West Wing were TV shows that our husbands were not interested in, which we loved and tuned into together. When the Ally McBeal series was televised in both the UK and SA, we watched the episode and then phoned each other to discuss it.

Maria picked us up from the airport and dropped us at the Robertson Small Hotel, with the expectation we would see them that evening. The hotel was five-star, very upmarket with its own swimming pool, luxurious ensuite rooms and good service. It was a treat as we didn't stay in hotels often. It enabled us to sleep and get our bearings before we had to get ourselves settled into Robertson again. Robertson was a small mostly Afrikaans (descendants of Dutch settlers) town. Our house was on the next street from the hotel. Maria lived two streets away. There was a high street with shops, two supermarkets, numerous churches and several bars.

Our first few days back in South Africa had to be spent in reawakening our life there. Every year I had to go to the bank personally to reactivate my bank card, just across the road from the bakery, which sold the best milk tart in the town. This year I had to inform the bank that we would be crossing the border and using our debit cards. They gave me instructions to accomplish this.

Our apartment on Hope Street had to be transformed to a liveable space. It was a converted garage. When not there it housed the bakkie but on our arrival the vehicle was moved to the driveway. The double bed was brought down from its stand-up position and the duvet and pillows shaken out of their black bags. The camping chairs were brought out and the TV had to be reactivated with its satellite box. Turning on the fridge and recalibrating the hot water system completed the yearly tasks.

Greeting our new tenant in the main house and assuring her of continued privacy had to be done immediately. The tenancy agreement and day-to-day management were handled by a local agent. This tenant kept the main house clean and was responsible for keeping the garden tidy. Paying the rent on time contributed to her being an excellent tenant.

Our tradition on our first night in South Africa was always to have a braai at Sandor and Maria's house with boerewors, South African sausage. Syd washed this down with a Castle Lager, and we enjoyed this as the temperature dropped from forty degrees to a comfortable twenty.

All this was interspersed with shopping and lunches out with Maria. I slipped into her life. Getting up at 5am for an early morning swim wasn't the highest on my list of great things to do but I went because that was part of her routine. The heat meant that South Africans had a different routine to us. They got up early completed some tasks and rested in the afternoon and came alive again in the evening.

Syd did not escape Maria's attention. He was pulled into the hospice to give a fire safety management course for the caregivers. The highlight was setting off the extinguishers, a practical and entertaining moment for all. Maria had a knack for using all resources to further the best practice of the hospice and those included humans. She wanted to introduce us to some of her private clients, like the wedding event centre and of course the hospice. The donkey sanctuary near McGregor, employed her as a management consultant for two days a week, and was on the itinerary for a visit. This allowed us some quality time to spend together, without our husbands.

Eseltjiesrus Donkey Sanctuary was a pleasant detour from everyday life. The mountain backdrop, with a few bushes and trees dotted in the foreground made this spot very scenic. The scrubland yielded red earth intermingled with the grass and gave the place a scorched-earth appearance. There was plenty of space for the donkeys to roam in their little groups.

As we parked the car, there was still a fresh breeze, yet the morning promised a hot finish, up to thirty degrees. There was a slight whiff of donkey dung, but it was not overwhelming. Shade cloth shelters provided the donkeys with a respite from the hot sun when they needed it. I was always used to plain grey animals with a cross on their backs, but here the donkeys came in all shapes and sizes.

I was particularly amused by two donkeys who roamed together. They had large, slim ears and a circular white blaze on their mouths, which made them look like they had dipped their noses into a bucket of paint. Maria had chores to do; making sure the water troughs were full and refilling the hay bags. She knew all their names and was comfortable around them. Not me. A sharp nudge in the back reminded me that these animals loved people interaction. I turned and stroked the naughty one. There was something calming about all this. I gazed at her beautiful almond eyes. Was she neglected or abused? The care these animals received challenged me about the care of children on this continent. So much was done for the care of animals, wouldn't it be great if as much care was lavished on some of the children of Africa?

Another donkey stuck its face into the shoulder of one of the workers. This one had an unusual reddish, fringed mane. Maria put a halter on another donkey and cleaned its eyes. She was so relaxed with these animals; I'm reminded of her horse-riding days, when it was free with the Naval system. She tied the halter onto a post and raised the donkey's hooves to clean them with a pick.

Besides the many fields for grazing, this complex boasted a Visitor Centre with a bookshop and café. We ordered rooibos tea and a sandwich, while Maria chatted to the staff who obviously all knew her. She showed me her office, a hut alongside the Visitor Centre, with a beautiful view of the river and gardens.

It was inspiring to be with Maria because she was so different from me. Visiting the donkey sanctuary was mother-daughter bonding time for us. I am a little withdrawn and not good at social chit-chat. She was as bold as brass, a little quirky and on the go all the time. She didn't care what she looked like. Wearing a triangle scarf around her head, no make-up and being obese gave her a rather odd appearance, but I loved her and made the most of my yearly visits.

While I spent this time accompanying Maria, Syd cleared the garden of a year's growth, using his bakkie to get rid of the cut-down hedges and branches. He noticed the vehicle was pulling to the right. This could be a problem. It would be alright if we were staying locally but a long trip into Africa meant the bakkie must be tip-top. What was the problem? Would we be able to get it fixed by our leaving date, Monday 3 April? Would the dealer have stores or would parts have to be ordered?

Dashing up to the local mechanic before he closed for the weekend, Syd discovered the work could only be carried out by the GWM dealer in Worcester, 51 kilometres away.

Worse than that the mechanic had pointed out that the car tax disc showed the tax was overdue by four months, which couldn't be fixed on a Saturday. In South Africa everything closed on Saturday midday and did not reopen until Monday morning.

Syd told me that the mechanic tested the wheel alignment and detected a fault, with the rocker arms. Our early Monday morning start was not going to happen. We had worked out our timetable with precision to reach Eugene for the beginning of the pastors' school. Would it still be worthwhile to go?

How much time would we lose? Would we get there in time to do some Bible teaching?

Nothing could be done but just to wait for Monday to come. So, the barbecue organised on Sunday was a pleasant way to spend some time. Arriving at Adderley Street, the driveway gate to the right of the house was open, so we drove straight in. Several cars were already parked along the four-metre drive which curved round to Sandor's workshop. An amazing display of bougainvillea climbed the border fence, the scarlet flowers welcoming a sunny afternoon.

We knew some of the guests already. Samantha a businesswoman and Craig and Jenny, the scientists greeted us warmly. I recognised the dulcet tones of Adele, "hello, it's me", inviting us to party.

Maria's dogs, five in all, scuttled round our feet adding to the madness. As I looked around, I reaffirmed what an amazing place this was for a braai. The grassed area, five by twelve metres, held enough seating for all dozen guests to be comfortable. On the far side, a huge palm tree gave just enough shade. It was the outdoor patio area which was the real gem. Purpose built by Sandor it contained everything for ease of outdoor cooking. A huge barbequing space, three metres wide and two metres high was ideal for the hot coals. There were two levels to cook on, so if a potjie was on the menu the huge pot swung forward on an arm to stand just above the fire. Alongside this space, was a portable bar which could be moved to the other side of the stoop. It stocked a tremendous number of bottles of Castle Lager, the South African beer.

The weather was glorious with wall-to-wall blue sky and an acceptable heat. Sometimes it was too hot but that day it was great. Several of the couple's friends had been invited, who we knew so it was a convivial assembly. Maria's voice carried over the buzz of the happy revellers.

"Have you checked with Naomi about insurance documents, if you are going out of the country?"

Suddenly Maria had thought of something I hadn't.

In this Afrikaans town everyone knew everyone else. Without prompting, I could hear Maria talking to Naomi.

Maria was very efficient but very annoying in taking our lives into her own hands.

"Naomi was still in her office. She'll get it typed, and you can pick up the insurance document before you leave on Monday." Maria said.

When travelling from one country to another in Africa, you needed to carry all your documents with you. We had South African passports as well as British and those were convenient, viz visas and taxes in the African countries.

"Yes, that should do it," said Sandor to Syd.

"Do what?" I interrupted.

All I could see was blocks of wood bound together. Sandor being technically minded and a bit of an inventor, knew what this was about. I didn't.

Sandor laughed as he said, "Well it is one step up from elephant dung."

Now I cottoned on. The blocks were to be tied around our rear wheels like thick treads. When we had visited Botswana in 2013 the bakkie had got stuck in soft sand for a couple of hours. No one had been around. Syd sent me off to collect elephant dung and sticks to put under the wheels. I collected the sticks but refused to get the elephant dung. I had no gloves. My anxiety level had gone off the charts. What would I do if confronted by a big bull elephant? After a few hours, a ranger came from the other direction and though reluctant, threw us a rope to attach to our vehicle. The dung and sticks did provide the right surface for our wheels to get out.

"People using this route usually have 4x4's, not trucks like yours," the ranger said.

That day there was nothing more to say.

We enjoyed South African boerewors, 90% spiced beef sausage, plenty of salad containing avocados from our tree in the garden. And of course, Castle Lager.

"Mum, I think you'd better give me the telephone numbers for those places you know you're staying at, and especially Eugene and Tina's and your route." Maria fidgeted with her hair. "Yes, do it now, please."

I complied. Maria would be our help if anything happened on this trip. I gave her all the information I had so far.

As I kissed Maria goodbye she said,

"You know you don't have to go to Mozambique, if you really don't want to."

## 4. Great Wall Motors

Our time schedule was tight. Syd and I seemed to be tripping over one another in nervous anticipation of another problem. I prayed and knew our Lord would help us through these difficulties one by one. That is how we tackled them, one by one.

We spent the first part of Monday 3 April queuing at the Traffic Department for our tax disc. It was a simple procedure but not automated, so we just had to wait. We then scooted to Naomi's office to get our insurance cover certificate, which was waiting for us.

Just before lunch, we set out to tackle the 51 kilometres to the central town of Worcester. It was a medium sized town but displayed some of the bigger stores that South Africa had. It boasted a super new mall, with a big bookshop, cheap supermarkets and a liquor store (off-licence). More importantly it contained the GWM (Great Wall Motors–Chinese) dealership where we could speak to a specialist mechanic about our vehicle's needs.

The mechanic was able to give the vehicle a quick once-over and pronounced track rods and ball joints needed ordering, which we were assured would arrive early in the morning and our truck would be first in the queue. Relieved a solution was on hand, we decided not to rush back to Robertson.

We treated ourselves to some fried chicken in the town centre before driving to the mall. The bookshop CNA caught my eye. I had found the tourist guide to Mozambique in the apartment, so had a framework to hang my worries on. Syd, preferring the supermarket bargains, would only waste a few minutes glancing at the books. A pile of maps hypnotised me. Again, I tried to persuade my spouse that a map could be helpful, but I was disregarded with a comment about our journey being on a straight road and the exorbitant cost of these particular maps. He assured me he would buy a good quality map for a cheaper price at a Mozambican service station. A fact that I would remind him of at my leisure.

On Tuesday we got up early at 6.30 am. Maria knocked on the door as we were getting up, with one of her annoying small Pomeranians. I like dogs, but usually they were medium to large dogs, animals worthy of the name. Rosebud, a white version of the breed, had an incredibly small bladder, and when she was emptied out of the soft sling bag across her owner's shoulder, she always reminded us of that particular trait of the breed. Maria was on her way to work at the hospice, so in this instance Rosebud was the only companion. Sydney Sailor the rottweiler, Noah the boxer and Whiskey the yorkie were thankfully at home.

Stony silence between us marked the beginning of our journey. We took the exit road from Robertson. I had left the rental DVD on the table along with Syd's tablet and the DVD player. We had to go back and retrieve them, hence the marital blip.

As we negotiated the dangerous, narrow, fast-travelling road to Worcester, my head reviewed our financial position. Handbag, 11,000 rand in cash, check. Nedbank credit card, check. Nedbank savings card, check. Standard Bank card, check, English Santander card hidden, check. Oh no, I realised I'd left my Caxton card which had American dollars loaded on it, in Maria's safe for security. I dared not mention it. We had already retraced our steps once. We arrived before the car workshop opened thereby being first in the queue.

First in the queue or not, the mechanic informed us that the truck wouldn't be fixed until mid-afternoon. What could we do for the next six hours? We couldn't wait outside the car workshop. It was in the middle of nowhere. Should we go back to Robertson or go to the mall and wait there? I phoned Maria, explained our dilemma and asked her to pick us up. I sensed she wasn't happy with another change of our plans and a 100-kilometre round trip. She despatched her intern, Mitch, in her car to help us.

Just before Mitch arrived, the mechanic came outside from his workshop. His news was that contrary to his first estimate; the truck would be ready in two hours. We couldn't believe it. We asked Mitch to drop us off at the shopping mall before he returned to Robertson. We didn't phone Maria. She would need a couple of hours to cool down. It was a waste of her intern's time and her fuel. It was pleasant to walk around the mall again in the knowledge that the truck would be in tip-top condition today. We managed to get a boerie breakfast at Phat Food.

This breakfast included a generous portion of boerewors (Afrikaans sausage) and was good value for money. As for reading material, at the travel agency, I picked up a tour booklet about Zanzibar. Maybe that could be our next trip. At least it could be one that included hotels and air flights. I managed only a quick glance at the tempting maps of Mozambique in the bookshop, before Syd whisked me away to the supermarket.

It was just after two o'clock when Andries Burger from the garage telephoned to inform us that the bakkie was fixed and he would pick us up from the mall. We arranged at which entrance to meet him. Ten minutes later we saw our bakkie driving towards us. Oh no, it was obvious that this young man did not realise that the back of the bakkie was full of our 'gear', the cab is a two-seater, and three people must be transported. We had expected a 'courtesy' car, as they would do in the UK, but this is South Africa.

"I thought it would be quicker to bring your vehicle. Otherwise, you would have had to wait at least another half an hour until one of our vehicles became available." Mr Burger greeted us.

"Andries, you must drive. My wife and I will squash into the other seat. It will be a second honeymoon for us." Syd laughed.

Syd's quick wit was lost on the Afrikaner.

We returned to the GWM dealer workshop and could start our journey at last, at 2.30 pm. A day and a half behind schedule, we headed towards Beaufort West on the N1 with a temperature of 34 degrees centigrade recorded in the cab. The air conditioning was not working properly. The state of the engine was tip-top, comfort score was two out of ten. We were on our way at last. Mozambique here we come.

We were two pensioners, so different in personality on our way to another country in a truck. If I hadn't become a Christian, I wouldn't have met Syd and wouldn't be driving along a grand highway in South Africa on my way to Mozambique. Isn't it strange how the decisions we make, may seem logical but inconsequential but can turn into lifechanging episodes?

*I'd been a Christian for about two and a half years, and I felt I needed to be a family. Of course, Maria and my dad and I were a family of sorts but that wasn't what I wanted. When discussing this with my sister, she said,*

*"Come down the pub with us, we'll find you a good fella."*

*"No," I said, "I think I'll pray about it. The Bible says something about you can pray for anything and God will give you what you need."*

*I went red, embarrassed as she laughed at me. Six months later it happened. I would call my first meeting with Syd divinely orchestrated. I was attending the local church whose membership was under forty with an average age of sixty. It was just like any other Sunday but as the service was about to start, a man walked in with a young blonde girl, and they sat behind me. I glanced behind but was focussing on the service. In a Pentecostal service it was usual for the congregation to repeat the song before moving on to the next one. At the end of the first chorus, I heard the two visitors behind me shut their books, but the congregation repeated the chorus, and they were confused. So, I turned around and passed them my open book so they could continue to join in. As a polite thank you was spoken, I looked at the man. To say it was love at first sight may be a bit of an exaggeration, but my interest was stirred. We began dating. More of that later.*

Our goal along the N1 was to reach Bloemfontein a good half-way mark, but our take-off had been so delayed we had no chance of making that. Our best aim would be to reach Beaufort West to stay the night and then make an early morning start. We were on a tight time budget. Would we get to Mocuba before the teaching week began?

Mountains dominated the journey through the Hex River valley. It was as if the earth was split at one time. The huge buckles appearing in the rock made it easy to imagine where the earth ruptured. It looked so splendid. It was a wide expansive landscape or as South Africans say, we could see the big sky. In the valley were hectares of vineyards producing the table grapes for which the area was well known.

As we entered the region surrounding Beaufort West, the fading sunlight endeared a blue hue to the mountains. Syd said it reminded him of Australia and the Blue Mountains. I had never been there. Perhaps, one day I would go. For me, it looked like the mountain was enchanted, like a fairy had waved a wand.

Beaufort West was the capital of the Great Karoo and the gateway to hectares of scrubland. The Karoo was chilly at night, but I was oppressively hot. As I looked at the cab temperature gauge it read 41.5 degrees centigrade. What was wrong with the air conditioning? Syd explained that when the air-con was on, the engine overheated and lost power and that is why we couldn't switch it on for very long.

A Theunis de Jong sky accompanied us through the ups and downs of the hills. The Beast, our bakkie, was complaining about the gradient. At last, we entered the town and saw a camping sign indicating seven kilometres to go. Our spirits were lifted. The signs took us out on the other side of the town, where we encountered a roadblock. The officer checked our newly renewed tax disc and Syd's driving licence, and we were soon on our way again.

We travelled down a dirt track with little sign of a camping site. The truck ahead came to a halt and turned around. We did the same. The fact that another traveller had decided this was the wrong route for him, indicated maybe we were heading in the wrong direction. There was no other traffic on the track in this remote location. No one to ask.

We continued slowly and saw an entrance to what looked like a nature reserve. The sign "Steenbokkie" indicated some level of civilisation as we crossed the cattle grid. Looking through the ungated entrance, we could see a building on the hill ahead and as we approached another sign "Camping" indicated we were on the correct path. The sun had set, and the darkness enveloped us quickly.

We had found a place to stop for the night. It was too dark to pitch the tent. Syd put a few things under the truck and in the cab to clear a space to sleep. The ablutions block was well-lit and easy to find. The campsite owner took our 200 rand (about ten pounds) and we could put aside the stresses of the day and sleep but not before we had driven back to town and eaten a superb supper at the local Spur. Syd had his favourite spareribs, and I had a chicken burger. Spur food was nationally revered because as well as your main dish being cooked very well there were a lot of accompaniments to go with it – chips, onion rings, vegetables and rice.

As we ate, Syd spotted a plaque with the information that Dr Chris Barnard, famous heart surgeon was born there and there was a museum in the town, dedicated to him and his life and work. Pity we didn't have time to go there. Amazing to think that such a gifted surgeon, and he did perform the world's first heart transplant in Cape Town, could be born in such an obscure place.

Waking up and appreciating the campsite in daylight was a wonder, like finding the presents on a Christmas morning.

Our view across to the mountains and town of Beaufort West was unimpeded. The farm had all sorts of animals on it– zebras, horses, rabbits, donkeys, steenbokke (small deer), and hogs. We heard shouting from a youth and looked outside to catch a glimpse of the "well-fed" Afrikaner boy chasing the family cocker spaniel and obviously scolding him. Why? On the lawn was the prize rabbit from the rare breeds' collection – dead. We decided discretion was needed and retreated to observe from a distance.

"Hunting dogs do chase other animals!" Syd said.

We were blessed to watch the sun rise over the distant hills; black in the early dawn slowly turned purple and then desert brown. Around us were a collection of hi-tech camper bakkies and trailer caravans the likes of which didn't exist in the UK. South Africans took their camping lives to a whole different level.

Open flaps revealed kitchens and food stores, fridges and freezers. On top were canopy tents with ladders for access. The drivers erected and refolded their equipment with practised precision and efficiency. One truck had towing arrangements. We said good morning to the driver. On the side of the truck his mobile phone number invited allcomers to use his services in the event of a breakdown. Often, we would be over a hundred miles between garages and workshops, so we eagerly took his card and were relieved at making such a contact.

"I camp for three months at a time and am called out every day to the most off-track places," he said.

Nine o'clock was not really an early start but by the time we had re-organised our night arrangements, cooked our breakfast and showered that was the time. We didn't travel far before we came to another roadblock. The officer explained that they were the national traffic officers and last night we were stopped by the local people. Both were doing the same job although in different uniforms. I suppose the fines went into different accounts. It seemed like five men digging one hole to me.

Our journey took us along two-lane straight roads, not unlike the UK dual carriage ways but without the safety barriers. Heavy lorries dominated this road. The mountains once more formed the backdrop for kilometre after kilometre, with scrubland on either side of the road. Occasionally a horse could be seen in the distance. The outside temperature was rising. We were constantly dipping into the cool box for cold drinks. Powered by the truck battery the cool box served our immediate thirst. The time constraints meant that we were unable to make frequent or long stops along the road. Frequent roadworks and traffic officers delayed the journey further. The Karoo was a flat dry scrubland. The only time Syd allowed us a stop was to refuel. I was fed-up eating crisps and snacks and demanded a meal. Soon we found a super modern building presenting a smart restaurant. Bloemfontein was a marker along the straight road, and we usually stopped there, so this pitstop was unknown to us.

My chicken panini was tasty. Syd did not fare so well. He had been enticed to order spaghetti bolognese by a chatty waitress. Disappointing was the only word to describe his meal. It was cooked pasta with a tin of tomato puree poured on it. There was no attempt to add any flavouring or mix the puree in the meal. This mistake was not easily remedied. Syd felt queasy. He had to grin and bear it. We couldn't stop again until we reached Kroonstad in the evening.

Previously we had found the Travel Lodge economical and convenient as we could not find the campsite. When we arrived this time, we found the price for a room had risen from 380 rand to 580 rand. Syd renamed the place "Crapstad" because after driving around for half an hour, he couldn't find anywhere to buy beer, and it was getting late. I laughed.

We persevered and found a site with rooms for the night and a large Pick 'n Pay (economical supermarket) just outside. We bought Savannah (South African cider) and Coke Light, and we were satisfied again. The room at "Kroonpark" was basic but we just needed a good night's sleep. We could accomplish that without unpacking the whole truck, which assured an early start.

The chalet had a good double bed with bunk beds as well which we didn't need, a shower and a small kitchen. The TV was black and white, and it seemed that ninety per cent of programmes were in Afrikaans or Xhosa. That was a good incentive to sleep.

We were able to park The Beast outside the dwelling which made us feel a bit safer as the vehicle was still loaded with all our belongings as it was just a one-night stay. We should reach the Kruger Park the next day, but it would mean another day's hard driving with few stops.

At last, I was able to take out my crossword book and try a puzzle. My spirits were always lifted by this simple task.

## 5. Cross Words

A field of sunflowers greeted us on our fourth day of travel through South Africa. We saw ostriches too, always a delight for me. Their long spindly legs were mounted on feathery bodies while their giraffe-like necks hosted ever-busy sharp beaks, pecking the ground for whatever goodness they could find. Quite unusual for this landscape, it was slightly cloudy.

A mixture of cultivated land and wild grasses bordered the highway. Birds flocked on the bridges. In the Lowveld there were no other perches. There were a few spots of rain as we saw a signpost indicating there were one hundred and twenty-three kilometres still to go to reach Johannesburg. Our destination was almost in sight, by South African travelling standards.

A landscape dotted with boreholes and their overground wind sails; we entered the land of a thousand plazas and their correspondingly expensive tolls to pay. There was an alternative cheaper route through the suburbs, which we declined. We couldn't afford the time.

Directions were easy. We followed the N1 until we saw the junction direction to N4, to Nelspruit. We took the route and immediately the landscape changed. No longer an urban sprawl, we saw goats and cows tended by their herders. The pylons formed an uneasy juxtaposition. Business infrastructure exploited simple country life.

I was disturbed by the realisation that the signposts showed the new African names for some of the towns. This had changed since we were last here, and it was totally unexpected. Where was eMalahleni? Our map of South Africa was out of date. Just a few kilometres further, I was relieved to read Bronkhorlspruit 47. I could find that Afrikaans name on the map.

We had been driving for over three hours and as I glanced at the cab temperature, 33.5 degrees, I realised why I was feeling drowsy. The air conditioning was playing up again. At the Onestop, muffins and coffee were a well-deserved treat. It was then that I remembered I had to make a phone call to Nedbank about taking my credit card out of the country. Authorisation was needed to confirm my card hadn't been stolen. I hated making phone calls. I couldn't communicate comfortably. Talking to a machine just wasn't the same for me.

Smart phones just weren't my thing either. On a trip, finances were crucial, and it was my responsibility, so I made the call. I often shirked out of making calls, getting my ace communicator on it, but not this time; he was driving. I glided my way through the several options dictated and got to a bank advisor.

I answered the security clearance questions, but when she asked what my cell (mobile) number was, I was stumped. I was good at memorising landlines but not mobiles. What was my number? I reached down into my handbag to find my phone and started to panic. Syd caught my attitude from the frantic searching noises.

"Where's my phone?" I cried.

"You're holding it." He replied.

Of course. I was on the phone. What a stupid woman to ask for my number when I was on the phone anyway. I had it written down somewhere as well, for just such a time as this. At last, I found the scrap of paper. After passing further security questions, we were okayed to use the card in Mozambique.

"I can't believe you just did that!" Syd said.

"Me neither," I laughed.

The changing scenery became pleasanter. There were the green fields of a golf course to my right. The Sasol Power Station was easily recognisable, and we recalled the time when we went by it on our way to my sister's funeral eighteen months previously. That was a sad occasion, especially when I remembered that her emphysema was mostly attributable to her smoking from the age of fourteen. It was heartbreaking to know she had refused to quit several times, when the doctors had warned her. Just before she died, she was heavily dependent on oxygen, and her quality of life was severely compromised. Why do we succumb to the very things that kill us in the name of pleasure? Twenty years ago, many people woke up to the murderous intent of nicotine and quit. Today the crisis is obesity and resulting diabetes and heart disease and yet we are eating our way to our deaths. Most of us cannot stop. Me included.

We continued on the main highway. I could at last get out my crossword puzzle. Usually, I was banned from doing them, as it was a solitary activity and Syd liked to chat. But this time, I read out the clues to him, and he tried to get the answers. It worked for ten minutes and then I gave up.

Welcome to Mpumalanga, previously known as Eastern Transvaal. The next service station where we stopped, Alzu was a treat to visit. Behind the service station's necessary pumps and shop was a mini safari area with rhino, impala and buffalo. I couldn't believe my eyes. My posh Canon camera was in the luggage, but I had Syd's small Panasonic in my handbag. Syd allowed me just ten minutes to get some shots.

Unusually for this section of the journey, roadworks again slowed us down. You could wait for anywhere from ten to forty minutes. These were usually directed by women with radios who turned the stop/go signs manually. This was part of the culture and quite interesting if you weren't in a hurry. The Africans were eager to chat as they waited to change the sign.

*At another Stop/Go, Maria turned up the music on the stereo, jumped out of the driving seat and started to dance. Several people in the queue did the same. They made a party out of the delay. It was so funny to see. Fingers pointed upwards and arms waving, joy abounded in the sunshine. No English reserve was present just African exuberance. After twenty minutes the road worker turned the sign to 'go' and everyone jumped back in their cars to complete their journey. She sent me the video.*

The next sign read Nelspruit 94 kilometres. Eugene instructed us to stop at the town of Nelspruit to make sure we had local money before entering Mozambique. He explained Mozambique was a 'cash' society. Cards were not accepted anywhere for food or accommodation. You could withdraw cash from the auto bank machines. Eugene estimated that we would need to change five thousand rand (£250) to have enough for accommodation and fuel to get us to Mocuba. The Bidvest Western Union was situated in a mall at the beginning of the town. We missed the signs and drove up and down the main street twice before we could find it. More precious minutes were lost. When we entered Bidvest, we were stunned to hear that there were no Portuguese meticals to buy. The Mozambican currency was so unstable, visitors couldn't change rands into meticals at an ordinary bank; hence we went to Western Union. We were informed that Bidvest only sold meticals when it had managed to buy some from returning South Africans. We couldn't even order the currency. I was ready to turn around and go home.

Having the correct currency and enough of it was a sure way to avoid starvation, robbery and to make your journey comfortable. I had never entered another country without the correct currency or the means to get it. It was unthinkable.

As we exited the office, we exchanged a few words with an African who laughed and said, "If you have dollars in Mozambique, you're a rich man." Was this a word from the Lord? We had some American dollars in notes besides those loaded on my Caxton card, which had been left in Robertson. We decided to contact Eugene to ask for his advice. It was pretty scary. Something was wrong again with the network, and I couldn't get through to him. I was still using my English SIM in my English phone. I got through to Maria on the South African phone and explained the situation with the currency. Contacting Eugene on her phone she was able to get a solution for us from him. He said,

"Fill up on fuel at the Letaba rest camp on the South African side of the border. Then make for Xai-Xai and withdraw money from the ATM there."

This sounded precarious. We would be taking a chance that we wouldn't run out of fuel or break down with no money. Should we cancel the trip? Maybe just the Mozambican bit? We could still go to Kruger. The light was fading, and we had to reach the Kruger Park by 18.00 before the gates closed. I looked at the map and tried to estimate which gate would be the quickest. I decided on Malelane. I had been there before but couldn't remember the exact route. We had to rely on the old map. After a couple of accidental detours, we arrived at the gate at 17.50. The gate guards were very sympathetic and allowed us to enter the park but restricted us to the nearest rest camp at Berg-en-dal. We were not allowed to drive further than that. It was thirteen kilometres more to drive. The rest camps were fenced and gated and everyone had to be inside at night. We were so exhausted.

There was a rhino just at the rest camp entrance. I was so tired I did not appreciate what I was seeing. The Lord blessed us with this magnificent animal to begin our safari, but exhaustion prevented me from appreciating it. A rhino was a comparatively rare sight in Kruger.

It was too late to put up the tent. We were not the only ones to make an entrance to the park at the last minute. The campsite was very full, and we could barely find a place for the tent anyway. There were no braai (BBQ) places available, so our evening meal was restricted to the few cans we had. When I discovered we had the incorrect fitting for the electric hook-up, I wanted to scream. We wouldn't be able to charge our phones or use my hairdryer. But we had reached the Kruger Park. We put our camping equipment under the truck and clambered into our bakkie-bed.

It seemed as if everything was against us. Should we give up or go on? As you would expect, Syd and I disagreed.

## 6. God's Solutions

God always has a third option – something our small minds cannot conjure up. When we pray, we often have a solution in our mind, but God's solution to our problems is often something we haven't thought of. Sometimes the way forward seems blocked, as in our progress to reach Eugene and Tina in Mozambique.

The situation reminded me of another stalemate when Syd and I first met. He was so aggrieved when his ex-wife ran off and left him and three children; he said he would never marry again. As a Christian, my only option to further a relationship was to marry.

*Something happened in Syd's situation which made him realise everything was not going well for him to grow as a Christian. Indeed, there was a real possibility he could end up in prison. He and his children prayed that God would remove something in his situation. I won't give more detail because that is his story and maybe he will write it one day. The next day in the post, Syd received an offer from the South African Navy to take a post in South Africa. How did they know he had recently come out of the British Navy? Instead of removing something from Syd's situation, God had decided to remove Syd from the situation instead.*

*That night after praying and asking God was this the answer to his prayer, Syd had a dream about an island with seals on it. He got a map and looked up Simon's Town, the naval base in South Africa. His map showed an island near Simon's Town called Seal Island.*

*The following morning, he went to his daughter Natalie's room and saw a bible lying on the bedside table, Pleading with God, to know was this job offer from Him, he threw the Bible on the bed, and looked to see what the verses said. The Bible opened at Jeremiah 24:1b-7 NIV, and it read,*

*"This is what the Lord, the God of Israel says, Like these good figs, I regard as good the exiles from Judah, whom I sent away from this place to the land of the Babylonians. My eyes will watch over them for their good, and I will bring them back to this land. I will build them up and not tear them down; I will plant them and not uproot them. I will give them a heart to know me, that I am the Lord. They will be my people, and I will be their God. And they will return to me with all their heart."*

*On reading this, Syd knew God was sending him to South Africa through this job offer. He answered, yes, he was interested in the position. Then he told me about it and declared he was going to South Africa, with his children.*

*I was stunned. There was a lady from South Africa on the education course I had recently completed. She told me about the racial discrimination and what the country was like. Her husband had been imprisoned on Robben Island and when released after a couple of years they had been deported. She had been teaching in South Africa, but her qualifications weren't recognised in England, so she had retrained.*

*I got on well with Ursula, probably because we were both mature students and had children. I had no reason to disbelieve her description of her life in South Africa. It didn't seem like the place I wanted to go to.*

*"Well, do you want to come with us to South Africa, Rosalie?"*

*I was stunned not flattered. There was not even a hint of a marriage proposal. In fact, I was tempted to think Syd may have been looking for a housekeeper with benefits. No, maybe he wasn't. I had to make my Christian stand clear.*

*"I can't take my daughter to the other side of the world to a disreputable country without being married," I said.*

*"Well," he said, "I don't want to get married again."*

*"I don't really want to go to South Africa. I've heard from my friend at college that it isn't the sort of place I want to be associated with. They have race rules that I don't agree with."*

*"I went to South Africa with the Royal Navy, and it isn't quite like it is portrayed on the TV, you know."*

*After a brief silence when neither of us knew how to break the stalemate, Syd said,*

*"Okay, if we get married, will you come?"*

*We were both crossing borders, doings things we didn't really want to do. Syd didn't want to get married again. I didn't want to go to a racist country like South Africa. God's solution forced us to reappraise our previous convictions.*

*"Yes, I will."*

*I was still apprehensive. How would I fare in a strange country as a naval wife with three stepchildren and my own daughter? How could I cope with so many children?*

But I did cope. Looking back now I realise how hurried and sometimes chaotic our lives were from that day for each one of us. We never had time nor money for holidays or weekends away. We were all just surviving. Is that why the African landscape holds such magic for me? It is a different landscape culture—wide open spaces and lots of them. To say the sunny weather was better than England is such an understatement. It was hot often dry and dusty for days and days. Sunshine gives me a happy feeling, a devil-may-care attitude. It's like going through the Narnia wardrobe. In a way that's what the thought of marriage did for me. From the shame of a single divorcee with a child, I was embracing the respectability of family.

Our immediate circumstances called for trust in God, as when I was going for that emergency caesarean for Sam's birth. If Syd wouldn't budge, then I also had to dispel the fear and anxiety of something which hadn't happened yet. I prayed and felt less anxious. Perhaps the answer was just to plod on and deal with the emergency when it actually happened instead of worrying about it beforehand. That was Syd's method of living.

# 7. The Kruger National Park

The next day of our Mozambican trip, Friday 7 April 2017, we started early at 07.05. I was sad now that I hadn't taken more notice of that black rhinoceros we encountered on our way into the park. An amazing beast on the endangered list and I didn't appreciate it. I was so tired and just didn't expect to see anything apart from springbok and impala that close to the gate of the rest camp.

My hope was to be able to take some successful shots especially near Skukuza if we stayed at that camp. As we discussed the day's plan, it was obvious that Syd saw Skukuza as a quick pit stop and not an overnight stay. He wanted to head north and reach Letaba for our border crossing. For Kruger groupies it is well known that this huge landmass has different geographical microclimates where you would experience specific groups of animals. For example, at Berg-en-dal you would expect to see rhinos and as you moved north you expected to see the big cats around Satara. Further north you may see wild dogs. Letaba was not a hotspot for the animals I wanted to photograph. Syd was right in that the speed of vehicles was restricted, and as the park was so huge it took a long time to get from one rest camp to another. I could understand his reasoning and why we just had to keep driving.

I was disappointed. The original hook to go to Mozambique was wrapped up in my desire to spend time in the Kruger Park, now it looked like we could only drive through without stopping. Our goal seemed to have changed. Our mission now was to reach Mocuba on time. It was not a less worthy goal, but it differed from what I expected.

The open plain afforded clearer visibility as two huge male giraffes ambled from treetop to treetop to enjoy the higher branches other animals couldn't reach. Their ginger neck frills fluttered softly in the light breeze, before the heat of the mid-morning took hold. Red-billed oxpeckers did their work enthusiastically and pecked almost unnoticed. It was still early and the compulsory 50kph (30mph) enabled a good view as we made our way north.

There was little traffic on the two-lane tarmac road. In the distance I spotted a solitary hyena, too far away for a good photograph. We watched him as he limped furtively across the grassland, in no particular hurry.

For an hour we didn't spy anything in particular but then a group of six elephants appeared mysteriously in front of us as we went round a bend. Last to cross the road was a mother and baby. The mother used her body to protect her young one on her far side and once again my photo shot was obscured. What a joy though to watch the trunk-to-trunk communication between them.

Animals act as a mirror to human life and relationships. The elephants had reminded me of my family, of Maria and my other children. God had blessed us indeed. I had a deep sense of gratitude to God that I was able to experience this amazing park. My sense of the awe of nature was deepened. I was ashamed that I had complained so much about not having my needs met. We didn't have any Mozambican currency, so what? Wasn't this what many missionaries went through all the time? What about George Mueller who prayed in the food to feed ten thousand orphans in his lifetime. He didn't know what would happen the next day. We just have to trust God for this day, something I still hadn't quite mastered. Tomorrow would take care of itself.

We stopped at the Skukuza rest camp, the largest one, situated on the southern bank of the Sabie River. We readily ate a breakfast snack. Coffee was welcomed. We got into conversation with other travellers about our forthcoming border crossing.

"You know that if you want to cross the border from Letaba you must stay the night at the rest camp. It's the rule!" said one brash woman.

"We didn't know that. Thanks for telling us," Syd said.

"Last time I had to wait ages at the border. There was a problem with my car documents," she continued.

"So, what was wrong with your documents?" Syd asked, anxious we wouldn't have the same problem.

"Oh," she laughed, "Silly really, it was the company car and therefore I wasn't the legal owner. I suppose it makes sense." As we owned our vehicle and had the correct documentation, we shouldn't have that difficulty. In another message of doom, she related weather problems. When she crossed, it was so wet the terrain was difficult to navigate. It had been dry for quite a while so we didn't expect such a problem.

After a much-needed toilet opportunity, we headed for the Satara rest camp, the camp of the big cats, further north. I remembered the busy, popular rest camp from the previous year. Then we were lucky enough to see an amazing leopard sitting in a huge baobab tree. I had plenty of time to photograph it and got some brilliant shots which were now proudly sitting in a frame on my bedroom wall. Another sighting we had was of a lion with its kill, being watched by a hungry crocodile. Quite unusual in a photograph but amazing in the wild. Having time to observe nature play out its daily activities while you watch, was a delight. People have become so desensitised after watching hundreds of National Geographic videos, they think it's just the same in real time. The beating sun overhead and the sound of animals in the bush and the nearby water add to the whole picture but cannot be adequately reproduced by my words.

Being late in the day our expectations of seeing animals weren't great, so the blue wildebeest were welcome. The huge herd of over fifty animals nibbled the grass of the savannah as we passed.

Their slightly bluish coats made it difficult to decide whether they were blue or grey. Black stripey shoulders and smallish, thin faces with horns gave them a rather odd appearance.

The road took on a reddish dust across it, as the baboons enjoyed the midday sun. A large troop with a couple of males but mostly females and babies, filled the road. We drove slowly but couldn't wait for them all to move, if indeed they would have. Baboons held no wonder for us as we had experienced their destructive behaviour in Da Gama Park when they would raid the houses and flats searching for titbits to appease unsatiable appetites.

We moved on along the road which bordered the Sabie River and were delighted to see hippos wallowing in the river. Just a bit away was a lone water buck looking so amusing with his white ringed rump.

During the 70 kilometres to Letaba we observed the cab temperature rise to 32.5 with alarm. I was glad to reach the rest camp. There were more disappointments that afternoon. Very apologetically the receptionist informed us that we could only stay for one night, because of heavy bookings for the Easter holidays. What could we do? It wasn't practical to drive out of the park and stay outside for one night, then drive in the next day. Circumstances were once more manoeuvring us against our wishes and decisions. We would have to cross the border one day earlier than anticipated.

At least we had time to set up camp for the night and rest. After setting up the tent, I decided to make the most of what we had and go for a swim in the pool. I had the pool to myself. As I floated on my back, I reflected on how fortunate I was to be there anyway. A quick movement over the water alerted me to put my feet on the bottom of the pool. What was it? I espied a kingfisher in a bush. How beautiful. God was with us. These other things were just blips in our plans and weren't really of any importance. There were bumps in the road of life. Though unpleasant they weren't the whole road. In the midst of this busy holiday time, I was privileged to watch the beauty of nature before my eyes and enjoyed it.

One ritual in the rest camps was to take an afternoon drive around 4 pm. It was then the animals were waking up and coming out to enjoy the evening, just as we were. Very early morning was the other favourite time for good sightings. Syd being practical, suggested we drive along the road to the border (26 miles). So, we did. A big herd of elephants emerged from the bush in front of us. It was too dangerous to drive through them. We waited, admiring this family group.

Syd was happy he knew the route to the border post. The signs had been easy to follow. We returned to the rest camp just in time for the 6pm-closure. We took the opportunity to start our BBQ in one of the purpose-built brick braai-plekke (barbecue places). After pleasant conversation with the other campers, we enjoyed our pork chops and accompanying salad. We slept in the safety of our bakkie, after enjoying a boxset played on the DVD player.

The last part of the journey in South Africa had been stressful with problem upon problem. *I thought about the difficulties we had encountered in 1981 as we completed the necessary forms to emigrate to South Africa from the UK.*

*For any other family it would have been more straightforward but taking children out of the jurisdiction of the UK required permission from both parents. This wasn't just a holiday but a three-year contract. Even though Syd had custody, care and control of his children and they were living with him, he still needed permission from his ex-wife, and she refused. She didn't want them to leave the UK although astoundingly she had no plans for their future.*

*Two dates were given for a court hearing, August 11 and 13. The court proceedings were long and complicated and can be found in another publication. The court gave permission for the children to go to South Africa. We got married on the 12 August. On 13 April 1982, Maxine aged 15, Natalie aged 10, Michael aged 5 and Maria aged 11 accompanied us to a new life in South Africa. I was five months pregnant.*

Regarding this border crossing, we had managed to fill up with diesel, as Eugene had suggested. The next day, we would start a novel experience - visiting another African country. Syd was managing to live with cancer. It was amazing to see how driven he was. He would get us to Mocuba. Of that I had no doubt.

It was a restless night for me. Disappointment mingled with a knowledge of the necessity of getting going on the road to Mozambique. The heat influenced my choice to sleep on top of the duvet. The temperature dropped during the night, so I dragged the duvet over me.

"Hey," I heard a shout. "Don't take the cover!"

"But I need it," I squealed.

"Use the bit you're lying on" came the quick-witted reply.

The joy of camping! As we packed, Syd noticed the ants had buried the cord of the cool box. Amazing! Maybe it was a good thing that we weren't staying a second night.

# 8. Border Crossing

We knew this journey upcountry in Mozambique would be an arduous one, so we made an early start, 5.50 am. Soon we were driving at the regulatory speed of 30mph on our way to the border. We could see a queue of cars waiting and a chain barrier had appeared since yesterday evening. We joined the queue and got out of the truck, chatting to the other travellers. We had no idea how long it would take.

We asked the other travellers what we could expect on the other side of the border. We were told we would have to drive at a good speed to reach civilisation. As I looked along the waiting vehicles, I realised that most were 4x4s, big vehicles with sturdy tyres. I wasn't sure we could do what they suggested.

The border crossing post comprised a couple of wooden huts, with no real indication of what documents you must show where. The first hut was obviously the emigration department of South Africa. The emblem on the side of the hut showed that. The only official on duty stamped our passports and wished us a pleasant journey with a friendly smile.

The second hut was the Mozambican Immigration. I was a little nervous not knowing what to expect. Would they expect us to speak Portuguese? The officials were friendly if somewhat disorganised and didn't seem in any hurry. At first glance, there was no system, but I watched the other travellers to see which documents they produced. The first desk must be immigration as the official was stamping passports. The second one seemed to deal with the vehicles.

Our vehicle had to be checked after presenting our documents. Our documents were in order, and no contraband was found in the truck. Someone in the queue had already told us you weren't allowed to take in your own alcohol into Mozambique without paying extra duty. We made sure we didn't have any on us. The man in front of us hadn't been given the information and stubbornly refused to part with his whiskey. We waited for our turn. The time passed quickly but in reality, it took us three and a half hours before we were on the road again. We marvelled at the lack of maintenance to the highway. This dirt track was littered with strange, wire lines. Maybe it was to deter animals from wandering over the border. We were cautious as we drove but that cost us time. So much for keeping up a good speed!

The firmness of the track gave way to a sandy layer which made us doubt we were on the correct route. The vehicles ahead of us had sped away leaving their dust. We were reduced to 50 kmh as we negotiated the rocks and large stones, but we eventually reached the exit gate.

We knew that we were still travelling through the park but on the Mozambican side, but there were no animals. We found out later that the animals had been eaten a few years previously.

At last, we reached the exit gate. Two guards were standing at it.

"Where are you heading?" one guard said.

"Mocuba." Syd answered.

One guard looked at the other one and they both started laughing.

"Why are you laughing?" Syd said.

"Oh, it is far, far," said the other guard and gestured with his hands.

"Have you been there?" I asked.

"No, no, it is far," said the guard again.

We continued along the road, again a sandy track with massive dips, which caught us by surprise. We were glad when we saw signs of cultivation of the land and fenced off areas. Small trees were dotted around but there was little other vegetation.

During the journey I stayed in touch with Maria to let her know where we were, mainly because if we had a problem, she would be able to help us. I switched my mobile phone off as we left South African soil, encouraged by fellow travellers. Apparently, this helped to engage with the new satellites. I switched it back on again but there was no signal. Our bakkie was slower than the vehicles ahead of us and we were catching their trail of dust. We slowed down. It was unnerving to travel so many miles on an unsurfaced road. It felt as if we had taken a wrong turn. Eugene warned us of this and said we could expect a better road when we reached Macia. We didn't have a map, so I didn't know how far that was.

"Where is the service station where we can buy a map?" I asked.

Syd didn't answer. There were no service stations as you would expect to find in European or African cities.

"If we had a map at least we could chart where we are," I said.

Again, Syd didn't answer.

At 11.15 with the National Park behind us, we saw a spectacular dam. How could such a poor country afford this? We crossed a bridge to an amazing view. The temperature had soared to 34 degrees. It was hot and we were forced to stop three times for cows crossing to the track on the other side. We knew we were in Africa because where else would you find a stunning bridge structure with dirt tracks either side of it, instead of roads?

We arrived at a junction with no signposts. Eugene had instructed us to turn right at some point, but was this the junction? We saw a familiar 4x4 from the border, turn right. We followed.

There were still no restaurants or shops, so lunch was a packet of crisps and a bottle of water. There were no signs of community or industry. A solitary child stood by the side of the road selling charcoal. Huge palm trees towered on both sides of the now tarmacked road. Speed signs appeared but made little sense. There was no obvious change in the area zones but a sign for speed 80 was followed by one displaying 60 in just a few yards. It was very perplexing.

As we entered Chokwe, we were surprised to see a single white face. We stopped to ask about our surroundings. This tall young man hailed from Wisconsin and was teaching at a local school.

"What do you do if your vehicle breaks down here?" Syd asked him.

"I don't do anything. I live here."

A strange answer but he refused to elaborate so we had to be satisfied and moved on. The road showed signs of deterioration, and I wondered if we would survive. It did get better but before we exited the village, a police roadblock stopped our travel. Again!

The roadblock was manned by a single policeman who said, "You were driving at 79kph in a 60kph speed zone."

"Yes, I accept what you say but how do I know when the 60 zone is finished? There doesn't seem to be any signs." Syd said.

The police officer pointed ahead of us and said,

"The zone finishes there."

We both looked to where the man was pointing. We couldn't see anything other than a grass verge. His thick accent made his English difficult to understand so we did not ask him to clarify. There was no speed sign. This officer was gracious and said he would do us a favour and let us off with a warning. We were grateful but still did not understand this system, if there was one.

We arrived in Macia without further incident. There was still no signal for the mobile phone. We had been driving for seven hours without a break. At last, along the main street, we saw a café where another family was sitting outside. It was a stylish brick building with white plastic chairs and tables outside. To my delight we stopped at the Sabores restaurant (Macia). The owner accepted our South African rands and gave us a fair rate of exchange for our order of cheese rolls and coffee.

The restaurant owner was very friendly and spoke English. Our first impression was a good one. We headed to Xai-Xai. I was disappointed that the main highway was not a decent motorway but an ordinary two-lane road. Progress was slow. An impressive road bridge signalled our entry to the town, but the dwellings were shacks with Movie Tel and Vodacom signs on them. Syd suggested that they might be selling airtime. I was not convinced, but we renamed that part of the journey, "The bridge over the river Xai-Xai." We hadn't lost our sense of humour.

As we drove through the town, I looked for a Nedbank. Unsuccessful. We saw a sign for Standard Bank which allowed us to withdraw 5000 meticals (about £60), We searched the town for a fuel station and were pleased that they allowed us to use South African rands. Thank you, Lord. But they didn't sell maps.

Just a few kilometres further and we encountered another roadblock. The policeman claimed we were travelling 76kph in a 60kph zone. We still didn't understand.

Syd got out and walked to the passenger side of the truck and I heard him say,

"We are missionaries. No, we don't have 2000 meticals."

Syd chatted in a friendly way to the policewoman. The man remained stern, watching them. The policewoman wanted to let us off, but the sergeant insisted we must pay. The officers were armed. I watched in the side mirror and took a photo. They started to walk towards the truck. I got out two 500-metical notes, showed them to the man and said,

"This is all we have. I can't give it all to you, then we will have nothing."

I offered him one note. He took it and waved us on. We were both glad that in Africa, fines could be adjusted without the paperwork.

We had been driving all day since early – 14 hours. I knew Syd was tired. I certainly was. The sun was going down. Driving in the dark was horrifying for us. People walked in the road. Big lorries with only one headlight ploughed towards us. Syd tailgated a driver who seemed to know the road. I was very anxious then at last I spotted a sign reading "St Antonio's two kilometres". What a relief. That was the recommended accommodation. We couldn't go further. Would they have a room for us?

We arrived at 9 pm. Our first night in Mozambique was in Lindela. St Antonio's was not a religious institution as the name suggested, but a guest house. It was run by a 62-year-old white Angolan, who reopened the kitchen for us. He had built his business up over 15 years but now he was ready to leave the country. We feasted on barracuda, chips, vegetables and rice. It was a Michelin five-star meal.

There was only one room left. We discovered why–the bed squeaked. At 635 rand (£40) it was great value. It was good to talk to the other guests. Everyone knew everyone else or a relative.

Our first experience of Mozambique had been gruelling. We have had to cover so many miles to reach the recommended accommodation before nightfall. I wondered if Eugene's instructions were made at a different time of year, so accounting for the different experience of daylight hours.

Crossing a border, both geographically and in life, is a memorable moment. The worlds on either side are not better or worse, just different. You do have to dissect the different cultural values and issues. That is what it was like for me as we crossed into Mozambique. It reminded me of the adrenaline-fuelled court experience as it calmed down to the reality of a new husband and family. Different rules applied and no one told you what they were, like the speed signs. I marvelled that at least the rules of the road and the signs in South Africa were very similar to those in the UK. You had to work them out for yourself but that was possible to do with perseverance.

We emigrated to South Africa on the 13 April 1982. That was another memorable cultural change in my life. The first thing that hit me as we emerged from the aircraft at Cape Town airport was the heat. A warm embrace as the six, soon to be seven of us walked across the tarmac to the immigration lounge. The leafy palm trees occupying the central divide on the dual carriageway spoke of difference as the naval man drove us to the hotel in Fish Hoek where we would be staying for a two-week complimentary stay until we could get permanent accommodation.

The following Sunday we took the train to Simon's Town to attend a Pentecostal service held in the local café. This small, friendly group of Christians welcomed us. The children were incredibly polite and respectful to adults. When we moved into a house in Da Gama Park, the naval accommodation later that month, they invaded us with goodwill and kindness, bringing pots and pans, mattresses, cooked food and love.

## 9. Palm Sunday 2017

On Palm Sunday 35 years later, we awoke to the sound of singing and celebrating as a parade announced its presence. As we looked out of the window, a kaleidoscope of colour: blue and red skirts, green T-shirts and bright cap scarves assailed us. Two young boys beat the drums they were carrying. The people were so happy, waving as they sang. The countryside was full of tropical vegetation. It was muggy. Bordered by coconut palms and lush grass, the road carried the parade of people to their church, as they waved easily obtainable palm branches.

Over breakfast, it was encouraging to talk to the other guests of whom there were many. As in South Africa, there was a lot of networking going on, swapping telephone numbers. Our first day of driving in Mozambique had been gruelling and more difficult than we had expected. We both realised now that driving at night was too hazardous and we were informed that if you did happen to hit a pedestrian it was a mandatory visit to prison. The roads and villages were totally without lights, the verges were ambiguous, and the population understandably blended into the darkness.

We set off as soon as we were dressed, frequently seeing parades of branch-waving people. We needed to fill the tank, so were relieved to reach Maxixe. This was the first time the owner of the fuel station refused to take rands, and we were forced to use some of the few meticals we had. We saw two auto bank machines in the town. We stopped. I tried both machines to withdraw cash. Both unsuccessful. The machines required a six-digit pin code, and both my South African and English cards had a five-digit code. This baffled me and was not something I was expecting.

At least we filled our coffee cups at St. Antonio's. Syd asked me to pass his coffee. Ever obliging I asked him,

"I've put the lid right for you. Which side do you want the hole?"

"So I can drink it without dislocating my wrist."

What a silly question! We both laughed and the journey seemed lighter. Passing a sign in Portuguese, we realised we had crossed the Tropic of Capricorn. I understood what a latitude of 23 degrees meant.

This was a well-trodden road, full of trucks and buses, with people hanging off the back standing on the running boards. Women wore brightly coloured skirts and T-shirts. We wondered whether they were going to church. It was Palm Sunday.

As we drove the temperature was rising and by 09.15 it was 33 degrees. The weather was becoming more humid as we drove further north. An hour later we were stopped by the police again to receive another fine. These men were heavily armed with AK47s. This time we didn't argue.

It was soon time to refuel again and although this service station was miles from anywhere the attendant accepted rands. A toilet sign urged me towards another disappointment. Porcelain toilets and washbasins were in abundance but not plumbed in. I looked for an appropriate bush.

We saw a sign for Vilenkulo east off the highway. It was 20 kilometres out of our way, but we were desperate to find another ATM. It was lunchtime and the temperature had reached 35 1/2 degrees. It was sweltering. Not having any local money was freaking me out but I didn't say anything. The Lord provides.

The road leading to the town was a single track and divided by a short hedge from the oncoming traffic. As we neared the town, we heard music from the people's cars and the vibrance of the seaside. Guest houses and lodges lined the road. We reached the main street of the busy town and saw the African market. There was a huge notice, BANK, and I scuttled out to try this ATM. The sign on the building 'International ATM' was promising. What joy! I could withdraw from both my cards and at last we had sufficient local money. Thank you, Lord Jesus.

As we drove down the beach road, a tempting sign appeared advertising lunch. I was so glad Syd agreed to stop and bought pizza and cold drinks. The guest accommodation sported splendid chalets and a beautiful swimming pool where we were invited to sit to eat our lunch. The owner came to speak to us and asked us to view his chalets, which were delightful Barbie cabins.

The conversation soon turned to our journey and the proprietor laughed at our suggestion that we would reach Inchope by nightfall. Syd was not daunted, and I too wondered if this was just a ploy to get us to rent a chalet for the night. We were both a little spooked by the warning of bad roads and the night closing in. We hastily finished our lunch and got on our way.

The proprietor, another Angolan, however, enlightened us as to how the speed signs worked. He said,

"There are no signs telling you when the speed limit goes down – only up. The trick is to look in your mirror every time you see the back of a speed sign on the other side of the road. As you pass it, if it shows the speed limit you are already in, it signifies 'end of zone'. And you can accelerate up to 120 kmh. But if you don't see the sign, never increase your speed. The Dutch supplied 150 handheld speed cameras, and the police love them. They were a tremendous source of income for the country and more so for corrupt police."

I felt glad that at last we knew how this speeding system worked. We would be more careful.

Driving along Syd said quite suddenly,

"I think you'd better write down the names of the villages as we drive past the signposts. If we break down, we won't know where we are."

Yes, I was thinking the same. The decision not to get a map was, in hindsight, foolish. Syd explained that at the time I had mentioned about a map, he didn't realise that there would be so many small villages in between the major towns. There were no service stations on the route selling maps, just random fuel pumps. I grabbed my notebook and pen. I said,

"So, I was right about buying a map?"

No answer.

My task wasn't easy as Syd had to keep up the speed. African names were difficult for a European to spell so I had to settle for an approximation. Lord don't let this truck break down.

The road was marked by heavy, thick black streaks. Syd said,

"You can see that was a steering arm collapsed on a vehicle. Hm, I'm glad we had the steering done."

I said nothing.

Two soldiers with machine guns were waiting as we approached the Rio Save bridge. We slowed down. Syd spoke politely,

"Good afternoon."

"Good afternoon, Tata (daddy)" one soldier said.

A few questions and answers established our destination and reason for travel. The conversation continued about the hot day and the thirsty work the soldiers have. The word "refreshers" was mentioned. After relinquishing two bottles of water, we were allowed to continue. Eugene had warned us about the frequency of this happening in Mozambique and told us to carry single bottles of water. This we had done.

A flash burst of rain refilled the potholes, and we were stopped again. We were ready this time and handed out another two bottles of water, with a smile.

As the light began to fail, Syd stayed close behind another vehicle who seemed to know the road. A third vehicle latched on to us. Our trinity negotiated numerous pedestrians and animals in the road, as the sun set. Suddenly the potholes seemed more dangerous, and anxiety hovered over us. How far was the next accommodation?

At last, we saw the sign for the Iris Motel. Ignoring Eugene's plea to try to drive a further 50 kilometres, we stopped. This is the infamous "Roach Motel" named for obvious reasons. Nobody spoke English. We were shown a tariff sheet and the proprietor pointed to the figure of 2500 meticals (£50). We couldn't believe this extortion. I wondered if it was a special 'tourist' price. We had to pay because we could not drive one yard further. Making light of it, we carried our luggage to the room. Then it was time to explore.

The complex was large, about an acre and well-lit inside high walls. An armed gate guard stood on duty. There was a mini theme park, and we understood that this was a weekend retreat. The door to our room was under a porch and surrounded by a naturalist's heaven of bugs. There was a whole ecosystem on the wall attracted by the light and of course cockroaches. Inside, it was clean but the aircon did not work; wires hanging off the wall. Syd enjoyed watching local news and was irritated to find the TV was broken. Every part of the room appeared to need repair. We viewed the shower and toilet. The doorframe was busy being eaten by termites; a pile of sawdust leant against the bottom of the frame. I turned the shower on, and the showerhead fell off. Syd fixed it. I turned the shower on again. This time there was no temperature control. The water was scalding. I tried the sink; there was no hot water.

Syd checked the sheets and under the bed. Mosquitoes were in evidence but there were no large creepy crawlies. We covered ourselves in anti-mosquito spray.

The bar was empty, but the beer was cheap. We ordered a light meal in the bar and then retired, determined to make an early start. This route had been surprisingly brutal. There were few hotels and no campsites. The room was grimy, poorly lit and the shower was broken. The bad roads meant it was taking a long time to travel a few kilometres. This highway would never be forgotten. It is the one where I broke down in desperation at the potholes and vowed that this was my last truck trip in Africa.

Metaphorically speaking though, this was only a bump along the Grand Highway. Wasn't it part of my quest to understand just what a missionary is; to explore brave new worlds and to boldly go where few have gone before? It was just a blip in the grand scheme of things.

## 10. Mocuba at Last

We left the creepy place at 6 am. It wasn't soon enough. On a practical level, there was no hairdryer, so I left with damp towel-dried hair. No style. Temperatures were already at 25.5 degrees. As we walked over to our parked truck to put our overnight cases in, an African approached us for a lift to Gorongosa village. Where was he going to sit? The cab was only a two-seater, and the back was absolutely chocker, full of camping equipment, which we hadn't really used. Sorry mate, no room.

Ten minutes later, we exited the gate and saw the same man standing on the roadside, waiting. Syd had compassion and stopped. He talked to the man explaining our lack of space and how uncomfortable the ride would be. The man agreed that sitting in the back among the gear, wasn't such a bad idea. Syd hurriedly pushed some of the stuff to one side, making a space, and the man clambered in.

The highway had deteriorated badly. The potholes were so huge, we were forced to slow down to five kmh. Now we understood Eugene's instructions. It just didn't seem possible that this could be the national road. Syd was forced to swerve from side to side to negotiate this disaster. I had never seen such a road. The potholes were huge, extending on both sides of the road with very little tarmac in between. We hit a flooded pothole. The bakkie dropped dramatically to one side; for an instant it appeared we might roll. We were stopped dead. I broke down in floods of tears, real fear. Syd slowly drove out of the hole, even he was shocked. He cracked a joke, as always, but this time laughter was beyond me.

The landscape carried skinny dogs, usually light brown, goats and chickens, some of which crossed the road in front of us. They were in no danger from us at our slow pace. We saw men wandering around with machetes and broad knives and wondered whether they carried these for work or protection.

The Gorongosa district was the home of the national park, but we had no time to stop. A pity I had heard it was a beautiful place of dense forest and exotic plants. At one time, you needed a security escort to go through this part of Mozambique because of the local civil war. Our hitchhiker had asked to be dropped off in this area, and he soon knocked on our cab window to get off.

The vibration of the truck affected my Canon camera. I switched it off and hoped it would revive later. It had been on the floor of the cab, not the best place for it but handy for taking photographs!

In this region we frequently saw people filling the potholes with dirt and then as we crossed their path, they held their hands out for money. That's fair enough, but they shouted at us when we didn't comply. Filling the potholes was a good idea for the first few people who got through but after that they just became a nuisance because they didn't hold the road and falsely proclaimed to do that.

A signpost, Caia – 150 kilometres, appeared. Eugene's calculations seemed to be incorrect. We wondered how long it would be before the road surface improved. We passed a service station at which we wanted to stop to refuel but when we noticed the attendants were refilling tanks by hand from barrels, we moved on.

We came to the toll bridge and had our money ready. As we slowed down, we saw there was also a police check. The police were satisfied that Syd's documents were in order, but I was nervous. I never knew what to expect and we knew these areas were under a shaky ceasefire.

We soon came across another service station which was a relief. This time we stopped. At Caia the road improved but we were still surprised by sudden, unexpected potholes. Our suspension held out. It was just a momentary jar that disturbed us, but after experiencing the Inchope Road, we were relieved. We arrived at Mocuba around six in the evening before the sun had set.

You have reached your destination.

As we drove through the gated entrance, students waved to us. They were expecting us, as were Eugene and Tina who gave us a warm welcome with lots of hugs. They have had few visitors in the past few years, and no friends had made the journey. We had only just got inside the gate when the Adventurer decided he wanted to see the Malawi border, but it was 160 kms up the road. As we headed for the border, I demanded we drive back to the safety of Eugene's enclave. All I wanted to do was be inside the compound, curl up and regain my sense of security and my nerves. I ignored the pleas about stepping into another country. For once I said, no more.

We settled down to our evening meal. Syd had brought boerewors all the way from Robertson in the cool box. It was a treat for everyone. As the light faded, I left the group to get an early night and prepare for the teaching I would do.

The following day there was so much to talk about with our hosts. We discovered that the Bible school run by Eugene rented the complex for the teaching week. There was a room allocated as a lecture hall and accommodation for the students. There was a rondavel for Eugene and Tina and one for us. The facilities were less than basic. In our rondavel there was a double bed, a table and a couple of chairs. Just outside was a concrete walled space containing the toilet facilities. There was a shower of sorts and a long drop toilet. No electricity meant the shower was reliant upon the heat of the sun. The toilet was a seat over a long drop, a pit of fermenting manure, full of creepy crawlies. The toilet seat and cover rested against the wall so it could be inspected before you sat on it. Then you could knock off the spiders. There were plenty of insects to keep us company. Eugene and Tina only stayed here a couple of times a year as they had a small flat in the town of Quillemane.

Eugene explained that they only had a further two weeks in Mocuba as they were moving to Nelspruit, South Africa to start a new phase of their missionary service. The mission organisation would be using them as pastoral counsellors to other missionaries in Asia and other parts of Africa.

We were eager to catch up on their family news. They had two daughters. Chantelle was living in Nelspruit and running her own Montessori school where she also taught. She was married with a son and daughter. Tanya had moved to New Zealand with her youth pastor husband, and they also had a boy and girl. Through God's goodness Eugene and Tina had managed to spend vacations with both daughters. My mind filled with horror as I imagined the horrendous travelling conditions they had to endure when they needed to go anywhere out of this region.

I asked Tina how many times they had driven this route. She smiled and answered,

"Sixteen."

Syd said, "Hey, Eugene, how does your ancient Mitsubishi 4x4 cope with the roads? We were shaken to bits."

"I have to renew the shock absorbers every two years," came the reply.

"But what do you do if you break down?"

"I stand by the side of the road, holding a tow rope and a fistful of cash. Someone will stop," Eugene said.

Eugene informed me that progress had been good with the student pastors, and he would be ready for me to do my part the following day. The PowerPoint presentation had been translated, and I would be sufficiently rested then. I was looking forward to it.

We spent the afternoon of the following day looking around the town of Mocuba. The African market was lively and colourful with the youthful roar of teenage motorcyclists, who we later discovered earned their living by carrying passengers on the pillions. Government departments were housed in modern brick buildings contrasting with the cubicles of household goods, where their owners were eking out a living of a few meticals per day. I enjoyed the cosmopolitan flavour except when a motorcyclist taxi wagged his finger at me when I took a photo near him.

I looked at some cotton material for Maria to make a skirt. The fabrics were colourful and the designs creative, but what should I get?

I also asked Eugene's advice about my phone not working, as I hadn't been able to contact Maria since we left the environs of South Africa. Eugene couldn't understand why the phone wasn't working and we both came to the conclusion that perhaps the answer might be to buy a Mozambican SIM card. Whatever else it lacked, Mocuba had plenty of mobile phone stores. Eugene had to buy the card because you had to have a local address. I didn't know why but hey presto, the new SIM worked. I was glad that once again I was in contact with Maria. I phoned her straight away. She was very relieved to hear my voice, as I reported we were both well and had met up with Eugene and Tina.

Friends are special. I counted myself blessed to have had several good women friends in my life. Yet experiencing friendship and fellowship on a communal basis was different again. It took time. Rubbing off the rough edges against others could sometimes be painful, hurtful and unkind but it was worth the effort if you could stick with it. To join a group where this had already taken place, was awesome. This is how it was in Mocuba that Easter.

## 11. The Missionaries

Teaching people about the Bible was always special, even more so in this African environment. The students were eager to learn and listened attentively. As I spoke, Eugene was quick with the Portuguese interpretation. I felt as if I were speaking directly to them.

I explored the four letters of Paul with the students. These were written while Paul was under house arrest in Rome. His situation of not knowing whether he would live or die made these particular texts vital in our understanding of Christianity. Hence Philemon is about the choices we make. Ephesians emphasises the blessings we have when we become Christians. Colossians is about who Jesus is in the context of the universe. Philippians is all about joy.

The student pastors had a book which contained guidelines for the study of the various books of the Bible. The presence of the Holy Spirit made these words of God relevant to each person. At the end of each session, the questions they asked confirmed their learning. I was satisfied that I had completed the task well.

The room was not large but contained 15 desks for the students to sit at and take notes. The usual commentaries and different Bible versions, often found in seminaries, were not available to these young men. I realised how privileged we are in the West to have these resources at an economical price. At the front of the room was the audio projector and screen. It was interesting to me that our methods were clearly a legacy from the colonial days, when the missionaries taught indigenous peoples. The Portuguese translation was not always understandable in this African setting. Eugene had to explain several points again to the students, where their texts did not translate well in their cultural context. The teaching was knowledge-based about the bible. We tried not to be patronising, but an assessment of our own behaviour was not easy.

The classroom was naturally dull. The walls were drab; the sparse furnishings were dark. There was a single lightbulb, lifeless, high to the ceiling. There were no sockets. An extension lead ran from the centre of the building to supply electricity to the projector.

Brightness in the room came from the pure white smiles of the men, their teeth all perfect and clean matching their sun-bleached white shirts. The contrast to the students' black almost purply tinged skin was stunning. The Mozambicans were darker than I expected for East Coast Africans but the melanin in their skin enabled good protection from the tropical sun.

The heat was oppressive. This made the body exhausted, but the evening was spent in pleasant conversation with Eugene and Tina, mostly about their experiences as missionaries. This was important for me because our hopes of being missionaries in British Guiana had been thwarted at the last minute. Although our label said 'missionaries' to England, it did not feel like we were missionaries at all. Here we are missionaries, or are we?

Maybe we could label ourselves as short-term missionaries for this trip.

When Eugene arrived in Mozambique, he had been with the Assemblies of God mission society but soon found out that they were prescriptive about decisions in the field. Eugene's powerful sense of calling and slightly stubborn personality clashed with them. They resigned from that missionary society but stayed on in Mozambique, relying on the personal support they had gathered thus far. They later came under the umbrella of another mission society.

As I reflected on Eugene's missionary work, I thought of my own experiences of mission societies. As a young Christian in the 1970s, I was keen to pray for and support missionaries in other countries. I was interested as our secretary explained the situation of the missionaries our church supported and what we must pray for. My ideals were based on an outdated colonial model, something which the modern world has striven to amend.

Twenty years later, I had studied the changing roles of missionaries at the University of Cape Town. The colonial model was no longer appropriate, and an eyeball-to-eyeball approach was recommended where the missionary embraced the other culture on an equal footing. Both parties could learn from each other. I had studied the works of Bosch and Miroslav Volf. This was what I had been implementing with my work in the Mountain View township.

When Syd was in the South African Navy, they were tasked with going to Cape Town harbour and help with repairs on the Doulos, one of the Operation Mobilisation ships in dock. I was surprised when he came back and told me that you could only apply to go to one of the ships if you were financially supported by the members of your own church. This was a new idea to me. You were not even allowed to pay for yourself. As I enquired further, I found that the idea of getting church supporting your mission work was common. I wasn't sure how I felt about that. It sounded to me like begging or using your friendships and relationships in the churches to get money for you to do what you wanted.

Our daughter Maria came home from a youth camp aged about 19 and told us she wanted to work for Scripture Union, South Africa, in their office in Cape Town as a gap year. In order to do this, she had to ask members of the church to support her financially. Again, it sounded like begging, and we said no. She must start her tertiary education without a gap year. The gap year had become a badge of honour for some young adults at the church's expense. Probably, we were very old-fashioned and hadn't seen the changes in the missionary world.

Eugene's missionary work was hands-on and practical. From the farm where they lived, he visited the surrounding villages where he prayed for people and spoke about the love of Jesus, much to the local sangoma's (witch doctor's) disapproval. Eugene was healing in the name of Jesus. Not long after that the witch doctor confronted him, cursed him and said he would die. Eugene retaliated, saying,

"The curse is on you because Jesus lives in my heart, and He is stronger than you. It is you who will be dead in six weeks."

Six weeks later the witchdoctor was dying and told his followers,

"It is the missionary who has killed me. You must avenge!"

The other sangomas in the district hired assassins, who attacked the farm at night, with machetes and knives. Taken by surprise Eugene and Tina had to fight for their lives within a narrow galley kitchen corridor. Holding a bar stool for protection, Eugene shouted to his wife,

"Go and get the dollars."

The previous week they had received this money from American visitors. Tina fetched the money and threw it in the air. As the attackers scrambled to retrieve it, Eugene and Tina were able to run to the neighbouring sugarcane fields to hide. They stayed there the night, listening to the attackers ransacking their house. Their worry was that their dog, who had run away, would ferret them out of the fields. They didn't know where the dog had run to, but he had gone to the village and worried the people until they followed him. Other villagers having heard about the attack, came to help in the morning. They paraded loudly banging drums and led by the dog, came to find the missionaries. The couple had been wounded in the attack, but God had saved their lives.

Eugene recounted how he had gone to the local hospital, where the nurse wanted to wash his wounds with the tap water which was running out of the tap as a brown liquid. He refused and was able to drive to Maputo and be airlifted by the Missionary Aviation Fellowship to South Africa for treatment.

Several nerves had been severed in Eugene's arm. Despite hospital operations, he still had a loss of movement and sensation in his right arm and hand. Tina's hand was broken, and she had cuts and bruises. They also suffered severe trauma. If it were me, could I have returned after that? I doubt it. They did.

*It reminded me of one dangerous incident when I was in the Mountain View Township in South Africa. I was leading the weekly children's ministry, and we were singing outside the hut. Suddenly armed police officers swooped on the area, firing rubber bullets. Contrary to popular belief rubber bullets are just as dangerous as the real ones. I grabbed three children and shouted to the other helpers, "run to safety". Refuge was found four metres away behind one of the shacks.*

*People were running in all directions. A bullet whizzed past my head, the noise from its speed. Children and women were screaming. The mothers later told us that if there was to be a drugs raid, the police would phone the community leader and warn him. This time there was no phone call because the Cape Town police and not the local officers led the raid. Strangely enough we did return the following week.*

There were financial implications to Eugene's airlift. The bill was R27,000 (about £2000 at the time). They could not pay but asked God for help. They received a phone call from the director of MAF to tell them that the bill had been paid from a special yearly fund for worthy causes. A blip on their life journey where God answered with a miracle. How great is our God!

The conditions we were living in at the Bible school, could not be described as comfortable. I can manage no bathroom facilities, no flushing toilet, basic foods, oppressive heat, spiders and scorpions for this one week but I couldn't do it for years, as they have done. Tina had to overcome her fear of creepy crawlies every day. We heard her screams one night as Eugene had to get rid of frogs in the sleeping quarters.

Two days later, the students had to write a simple exam on what they had learnt so we were free to have another look at the town with Bernadette, a Dutch missionary who was running an orphanage play school and eye clinic in the compound. She was the owner of the complex.

Looking at the colourful African materials for sale in the market, I decided to buy some for Maria to make a skirt.

The town was fascinating. The local baker was keen to talk about anything to visitors to his town. He only sold single loaves of oven-baked bread and was soon sold out. If you were a local, you would know to get there early. Bernadette cooked us a tasty lasagne for lunch. We met her adopted family of seven children, who were enthusiastic to have their photos taken. I volunteered to do that.

Eugene ended the Bible school with a communion service in which we were invited to participate. As we entered the hall the students were already harmonising in song. An atmosphere of fellowship and love prevailed as Eugene and Syd served communion.

In the afternoon, Bernadette invited us to attend the eye clinic she ran. Those old worn-out glasses you gave, had been graded into a simple format and after a simple eye test, Bernardette was able to give them for free to the waiting people. One old gentleman sat calmly in a big wooden chair as he read from the chart. He was so delighted to receive a pair of spectacles which improved his vision. It was a refreshing sight to see these African people who could never afford to go to an optician, receive our cast-offs. The gospel was being distributed alongside practical means of help.

The next day was Good Friday, and we planned to start our gruelling ride back to South Africa. Having done the journey on the way up to Mocuba it was torturous to know what lay ahead. We woke up early to an oppressive heat. The cold shower was almost welcome.

We took in a few impressions of what we had encountered here. We saw a snail as big as the length of my foot, whom we named Zebedee. The exotic vegetation and the missionary zeal to grow vegetables in the dry dusty soil, was a testament to faith and hard work in action. The book of James came to mind, as we reflected on the crazy, dangerous way of living, with four passengers on a motorbike and people standing on the tailgate of a truck, singing with no concept of danger. We saw the radiant face of Bernadette's assistant sitting next to an open fire loaded with sticks on which a pot was sitting, cooking the evening meal.

We heard joyous laughter from the orphans in the playschool. All the children wore the same, coloured overalls, a sort of uniform. It was such a pleasure to hear their bubbly chatter as their carers led them in some activity songs. Then it was time for them to go on the swings and slides which I could help them with. I could not talk their language, but play was the same in any tongue.

It reminded me so much of the ministry with the children of Mountain View. Children were the same everywhere. The parents were delighted, mostly single mothers, because we used teaching materials in English. In our age-appropriate classes we used Scripture Union materials which focussed on the life of Jesus. We had three qualified teachers besides the other helpers. All of us enjoyed this once-a-week session. The entire community appreciated it.

As we packed, Eugene came to ask us to stay for the weekend in their flat in Quillemane with them, inviting Syd to preach at the bush church for the coming Easter Sunday celebration. We were conflicted. It would seem selfish to refuse and yet another two precious days of travel would be lost. We had a deadline to get back to Robertson as Maria and Sandor wanted me to accompany them to the Addo Elephant Park in a few days' time. Do we accept this once in-a-lifetime invitation, or do we decline?

## 12. Easter Weekend

What a privilege to be asked to preach on the most glorious day in the Christian calendar - Easter Sunday. I felt the magnitude of it more than Syd. He took it in his stride. Eugene was really keen for us to meet the people of the bush church, which he had been associated with for a few years, just outside the town of Quillemane. We said yes, we would stay for the weekend.

Eugene and Tina rented a flat in Quillemane, a coastal town 20 miles away. That was our destination but, on the way, we would stop to meet the pastor of the bush church, Pastor Maritzio. Eugene warned us that he would take a left turn off the main road, into the bush, where there didn't appear to be a road, but we were just to follow him because he knew where he was going. That is what we did.

Pastor Maritzio and his wife Liliana started the church with ten people four years previously. Now there were 150 adults and 200 children in the church. Eugene told us the story of the day they had had to move the baptismal pool because a dead body had been found in it, and it was contaminating the water. Previously, they had used the river but then they had to keep an eye out for crocodiles. These problems seemed so bizarre, but they were true.

As the church grew, the pastor bought a plot of land to build his church. As pastor he was also expected to support his congregation financially as no one had employment. We were not able to converse with this lovely couple, but we smiled a lot, as Eugene explained about the Christian work they were doing. After an hour with them, we continued the drive to Quillemane.

The flat was a little dingy, but at least it had a plumbed in toilet. We were told that this was a 'Portuguese' toilet. This meant that when you used it, you could not put any paper down it. When the Portuguese left Mozambique, they poured cement down the toilet when told of their expulsion with only forty-eight hours' notice. The colonial legacy to African countries was often surprising. Mozambique was no exception. As we entered the town, we could spot products of this colonialism in the style of buildings and the broken-down infrastructure.

Tina and I sent Syd and Eugene out to buy some lunch for us, so we could chat and catch up. Tina, diminutive in size, was mighty in faith. She had been a quiet person in the congregation when I knew her previously, but I saw a new fire and passion for the Lord's work that I hadn't noticed before. It was an encouragement to me.

I had forgotten that it was Tina and her daughters who started the cross-cultural ministry to Mountain View township from the Presbyterian church in Fish Hoek by taking left-overs to that place one Christmas. I am sure we all have the urge to help the poor with this basic need, but rarely do we act on the sentiment. They did!

The spontaneous sharing of their food developed into a well organised soup kitchen. Volunteers from the Presbyterian church made soup and put their containers in a freezer on the church premises. Every Saturday lunchtime other volunteers went to the church, defrosted the soup and collected left-over bread from the supermarket in town, Checkers. Then they drove the five miles to Mountain View, the poorest community nearby to give out the soup.

*The township people knew they had to bring a bowl with them for their soup. When I joined the Presbyterian church in 1995, enthusiasm from the congregation was beginning to wane for the soup kitchen. The needs of the people seemed overwhelming. Congregation members, mostly women could not cope with seeing the desperate poverty of the people just a few miles from their own comfortable homes. Emotionally, they found it difficult to come to terms with this. For many this was the first time they had ever entered a township. God called me then to assist with this project. I and about 40 of the congregation started a children's work midweek, a Sunday service, a clothing-selling enterprise, and a food distribution project.*

An hour later, the husbands returned with hamburgers. In this town there were few "Western" facilities. I was aware that as we came into the town, we hadn't seen any supermarkets or fast-food outlets. We saw many bicycles and motorcycles, usually with more than one person on them. On every street corner there were vendors selling live chickens. Somehow, I lost my appetite.

Around seven in the evening, several of the students Eugene had been mentoring dropped by to say hello. It was wonderful to hear their stories of meeting Jesus and their growth in faith. Eugene's ministry in Mozambique was to encourage local people to start Christian groups and fellowships. He didn't feel God wanted him to personally evangelise the people but to encourage young men to do this work and support them in doing it.

On Saturday, Eugene suggested we take a drive to the beach, for relaxation. It was good to see our friends relaxing from the strains of the ministry. Mozambique was famous for its beaches, and we weren't disappointed. We parked at the entrance to a wooded park area and walked through to a popular restaurant. There were no other customers. Eugene instructed us on the modus operandi. We were to go inside and pick out the fish we wanted to eat. It would be cooked for us and then we would sit outside on the shaded tables to eat. The owner was proud to show us his fish, which I hesitantly picked out. We were told to go for a walk on the beach for a couple of hours and our fish would be cooked for us.

A cripple approached us for money. Having been warned, we didn't give any. There was a dependency in parts of Mozambique which led to the misuse of alcohol and drugs. We saw the same trend in South Africa. I was sad not to give but respected Eugene's advice.

As we walked along the beach I was struck by the beauty of this land, white sand stretching for miles accompanied by clear blue sea. We paddled along the seashore as we talked. A few miles away a fragile ceasefire between Renamo (anti-Communist) and Frelimo (Marxist) was holding but only just. The war was supposed to have been finished in 1992 but since 2013 there had been numerous flare-ups by the insurgents. We'd seen the accompanying aftermath of war in the burnt-out buses and debris along the road on our way to Mocuba.

We saw a community of about 20 Christians taking part in a baptism service, using the seawater for this sacrament. The day being warm, the congregation just walked into the water with their everyday clothes. There was something so basic and simple about it; the people were singing joyously as the white-robed baptismal candidates were dunked under the water.

This was a great opportunity for me to listen to Tina talking enthusiastically about their ministry. It had not been easy for her, but she testified about God's provision and encouragement.

From my own experience I could empathise with what it is like to go to a different country. I remembered when Sam was about 15 months old; I had a breakdown.

*Disappointment. Tight lips prevent harsh words or selfish pleading. I'd really been looking forward to some time with my husband. We never have time to be alone. He made his choice, helping at the kids' club on a Friday night. Again, I'm pushed aside. Again. A glass of wine to drown my sorrows. Baby Sam is fast asleep in his cot. This tastes good. Just enough bite to blur the edges of hurt. What about a party? One, two, three, four, five, six, seven, eight plates. What food is there? Two packets of Smarties between eight. Ping, the sound of a Smartie dropping on a plate, ping. My glass is empty. Glug, glug.*

*Half the bottle's gone. What else can we eat? My hair is too long anyway. Snip, snip, a little on each plate. Some romantic music.... thank you for the music, the songs I'm singing, thank you for the joy they're bringing, di da di dum, feeling tired, just another slurp, the couch is comfy. It makes sense* ...My breakdown was related to my situation. I had moved to South Africa from England. I had no support system, that is no sisters nor mother in that country and I just felt alone.

Tina's needs were simple. She had no desire for luxuries. There was still a strain upon her in embarking on a missionary life. The sponsors were faithful, and Eugene seemed to give money out to their mentees as soon as they got it in. She had been traumatised by the attack on the farm, but she shared Eugene's passion for spreading the gospel. There was still a male/female divide in the community. She shared Bible studies and sewing classes with the women, while Eugene mentored and discipled the men.

Yet the main drive came from Eugene. I felt that sometimes the strain of this type of work was greater on the support person than on the one with the vision. We met

Tina again in South Africa in 2019 when she was recovering from a mental health crisis at a Christian retreat centre. She was enjoying the time to recover, and it was great to meet her again. In our situation, Syd has been the support worker, and I have been the main minister first as an evangelist and then as an ordained minister. He has enjoyed this role and been a great encouragement to me.

Women were sitting on the beach area on plastic chairs with buckets of fresh fish at their feet. This was the local fish market. A group of fishermen were hauling in the catch in nets as girls sat on the empty fishing boat enjoying the sunshine. We expected the fish to be cheap. The price for prawns was definitely the 'tourist' price. We declined and walked away. It wasn't long before one of the sellers ran after us with a discount price. After Eugene and Syd haggled, a price was agreed, and they bought a bucket of prawns.

We strolled along the beach and chatted whiling away the two hours pleasantly and when we arrived back the good news greeted us. Our fish dish was ready. A gastronomical feast! A huge flat fish centred the table, accompanied by huge king prawns, salad and as many chips as we could eat.

In the evening it was a pleasure to meet two students whom Eugene had invited. Joachim was studying languages at the university, funded by Eugene. Antonio was pastoring a church in Quillemane. Eugene's function in the city was to encourage and mentor the Africans as they ministered to their congregations. What did the future hold for these bright-eyed Christian men?

Easter Sunday has always been my favourite day of the Christian year. It is an awesome day to celebrate the resurrection of Jesus. Rising early, 7.30 am, we drove to the Nicodala district to attend the church service at the bush church. We didn't know what to expect. We had been told that this group are financially poor but spiritually rich.

We drove to just outside Mocuba when Eugene signalled left, to where there was no obvious road. He turned down a dirt track and I was amazed he knew where he was going. After passing a few shacks, a sandy track appeared in front of us. It was rainy and I wondered if it would be muddy on the way back, already thinking about our exit route. We had heard stories of American visitors getting stuck in the mud. I didn't fancy that!

Ten minutes later we stopped. I guessed we were at the church. There was one thatched dwelling a little bigger than the other houses. Was that it? One congregant was standing outside waiting for the service to begin. Most of the congregation had already attended an early baptism at the river.

The church building was simple, about twelve feet long and six feet wide. Wooden poles held up a central beam and tarpaulin covered that. A lectern stood at the front and on both sides were wooden log benches and to the right front a huge blanket. Inside it was dark there being no electricity for lights only the natural light coming in from the door space.

The central beam had been carried on the heads of the church women seven and a half miles because the search for a straight beam had taken them that far. I looked at the building with a new respect, aware of the dedication it had taken to be erected. This congregation had been personally involved with the growth of the church both spiritually and physically. Their place of worship was important to them.

I looked outside at the big tree, its shade extending to a diameter of about eight feet. They called it "Sunday school". This was where all the children gathered to hear tales of Jesus. They sat on the ground and listened as action stories were told. Buildings were important but these people made use of what they had; in this case it was the big tree.

The congregation arrived in dribs and drabs. A myriad of women and children sat on the blanket, while 60 men and youths sat on the logs. The form of the service was very much what we were used to – worship singing, prayers and a sermon. The worshippers were led by a group of singers, a drummer and a shuffleboard player. We enjoyed the lively singing and excitement of these people. There were no hymn books. The songs were simple and repetitive; well known.

Syd preached a brief message from the first letter of John about sharing and love. It was time for Eugene and Tina to move on. The congregation would now have to share them with the other work they would be doing. The collection was taken up in a very African way. Placing a plastic bucket on a chair in front of the lectern, the congregation was invited to give. Many came singing to give generously out of their little. The collection was the equivalent price of one can of Coca-Cola. No one was employed in the congregation. Eugene led the communion after the collection.

Then there was a special farewell for Eugene and Tina. A lively youth group performed song and dance accompanied by the drums and harmonious singing. The children gathered to have their photograph taken. The four of us were invited for a special lunch.

We were ushered into one of the huts where we were asked to sit. Smiling ladies brought in the food. A huge plastic bowl containing pasta with a smattering of tomato sauce was on the table. In another bowl there was chicken still on the bone, hacked rather than cut or chopped covered by a greasy liquid. Syd with the constitution of a hippo ate heartily, while I just sat, with a queasy stomach. I knew the effort and sacrifice the people had made and was grateful, but I couldn't eat it. I put a bone on my plate and pretended.

Why is it my digestive system would not allow me to just eat anything like others? I felt ashamed and guilty. People had paid in money they didn't have, to make me a meal. They had cooked, probably on an open fire, to get the food ready. They didn't think anything was wrong with this food. They were probably proud of their efforts. I could not eat it.

We were eager to hit the road, but the congregation were just as eager to keep us. At 11.35 am we were able to make a departure. Discussing the return journey with Eugene, Syd decided we must stop at Catapur for the first night. This was a well-known bush camp, and within a reasonable distance. Tina asked us to make a booking for them for one night as it was only possible to book in person, not by telephone nor email.

We were grateful for the recommendation of a safe haven for the night, but wondered would we make it before nightfall? We were not sure what the entrance looked like as we didn't stop there on the way up. Would we miss it in the dark?

Being with missionaries for a week, I realised I couldn't have enjoyed being in their situation for 18 years. It wouldn't have been any different in British Guiana on the edge of the Amazon, would it? The poor quality of the road would have been exchanged for rivers and the difficulty of travelling on the Amazon. I suffered physically. Every day the bottom of my spine ached, and the pain radiated up my back. It would have been no different there.

The living conditions weren't just poor. After my experience of flushing toilets and hot water showers, how could I endure long drops and facecloth washes? Maybe it would be different if we had grown up with those limitations. It wasn't poverty I was afraid of. It was unhygienic personal indignity.

## 13. Mozambique

Even a blurred photo can evoke powerful memories when looked at again. That was my reasoning as I snapped pictures of the African culture as we travelled to the Catapur Lodge. The worst part of this return journey was the knowledge that we had to go back the way we came. There was no alternative route. The vision of that dreadful road from Caia to Inchope knotted and gnarled my tummy, so it was with some relief that this first part of the journey was uneventful.

At 1 pm, we experienced heavy rain. Visibility was down to yards, and it was quite frightening. The potholes filled up with water which meant at least we could see them. We struggled on and at last we saw the lodge sign. The buildings were well hidden from the road. As we drove in the estate, we saw it was like a nature reserve with plenty of birdlife in the vast wooded areas.

We discovered that the owner of the lodge also owned and harvested the forests. The lodge was a secondary business the main one being the timber on Anton's land. He revealed that he did not advertise accommodation but relied on word of mouth. At the reception, we made Tina's booking and moved into one of the cabins.

As we started to unpack, Syd spotted a gigantic spider on the ceiling. Worried that it might land on us in the night, we found a maintenance man to deal with it. He came to the hut with a broom and tried to entice the spider off the ceiling, but it only climbed into a crevice in a corner. Unimpressed with our anxieties, the African suggested we take another cabin because he could not get rid of the visitor. Without hesitation, we collected our belongings and moved on. I wondered what creepy crawlies we would have encountered in British Guiana. Generally, I was not afraid of spiders or snakes but was anxious that I did not know all the different species; which were dangerous and which were not?

The reception area contained a friendly barman, and several guests were enjoying a drink. We returned to our hut to unpack our pj's and then went back to the bar. The evening was filled with pleasant company, with whom we were happy to converse. The fire was lit, and we observed the people. One lady had brought her daughter to Mozambique from Zimbabwe for her holidays. Her husband worked for the parks board, but she wanted her daughter to remain at boarding school in Zimbabwe as the school was better there. Another couple had relatives in the UK. One resident of Mozambique talked about the lack of supermarkets and the fact that she could not get the spices she needed for her catering business. As I listened to this chat, I was glad they had the same problems as we had experienced and that the reason was a lack of availability rather than our ignorance.

Our accommodation comprised of a shared shower room and a bedroom. However, we could not shower because there was no water. We reminded the proprietor about the water, and he sent a maid who turned up with an empty bucket. We shrugged our shoulders. 'Diz is Afrika' would have been Maria's response to these types of problems.

A 6 am start saw us on the road. At last, we had learnt the lesson that you must rise early to reach the next accommodation along the road to prevent night driving. We knew this part of the journey would be potholes all the way, but we hoped to reach Vilankulo before the sun set. Numerous vehicles were broken down along the way. Rather unspiritually and selfishly, I was glad it wasn't us.

For the first part of the journey, we saw no people. Then a woman walking along with a baby at her breast caught my eye. She was also carrying a water container on her head. I marvelled at her resilience and creativity. A man appeared carrying a knobkerrie with an axe head. A live chicken squawked as the vendor swung it holding on to its claws. Soon the roadway supported men and women carrying hoes ready for work in the fields. Reminders of war, burnt-out buses, littered the highway.

Sturdy houses built of sticks and thatch were dotted on the landscape providing relief from the sand and broken tarmac. Potholes became pit holes in my mind. I began categorising the size of the holes. Lorries broken down at the side of the road became a frequent sight, their huge rubber tyres split in two.

As we approached Caia, now in daylight, it appeared different, scarier. The four-way crossing was difficult to negotiate. How did we manage on the up journey? Many over-laden trucks and buses surged forward, each trying to get its own way. Cars hooted, warning others to move aside. There was an easy comparison to Spaghetti Junction in Birmingham. Roads came in and out from every direction. You had to keep your eyes on your route and drive.

Guinea fowl pecked the water in the holes as we passed the Gorongosa National Forest. It looked beautiful and well worth a visit. There was no time. An hour's travelling brought us to women wearing brightly coloured skirts, with basins of freshly picked fruits hovering on their heads. Health and safety didn't exist here as mothers carried their babies on their backs as they rode on motorcycles and bicycles.

There was little wildlife here just a few birds. The rivers were dry. I wondered how Eugene could have endured travelling these roads twice in two weeks to sort out his passport issues after that attack. He told us he had to drive to Maputo in the south, more miles than this journey we were undertaking. Limping dogs followed the walking people. A whole family travelled on one bicycle. The man pedalled while the wife with a baby sat on the seat and a small child sat on the handlebars. It was too incredible for words but for these people it was everyday life.

I began to recognise some of the names of the villages. It had become chilly as the cloud covered the sky. We stopped at a garage to refuel, and the man had no change. We saw a roadblock up ahead. This time the men wore army uniforms. Syd slowed the truck and smiling they waved us on. We were glad they didn't stop us and gave a friendly wave as we passed but the sight of yet another AK47 had caused me to shiver.

The houses were slightly set back from the road, with fires burning, for cooking. Fields here were cultivated. More sophisticated methods of building houses could be seen. The walls were made of stones covered in wire mesh. Grass was daubed in the gaps. It reminded me of the wattle of seventeenth century houses in England.

Vendors along the roadside sold food with no appeal to me, in particular burnt corn cobs and not crafts as is common in Zimbabwe. This was not a tourist route. The countryside became hillier. The African people could be quite inventive. One interesting sight along the way was a sign for cold drinks perched on three electric freezers, which weren't connected to an electricity source.

I was still taking photographs but using Syd's small Panasonic. I wanted to capture the moments of interest of the daily life of the people. On this trip the scenery was so different in the daylight. But a photo cannot re-live the pain I felt as we continually rode over bumps and holes. Often physical pain struck my hips and shoulders, sometimes my neck and always there was that stiffness and pain around the coccyx.

After three hours driving, we stopped to check our wheels. We had heard some sort of noise which alarmed us, but it must have been something on the road. The truck was ok. We saw our first Mozambican field of sunflowers. How cheerful. This Gorongosa region was rich and fertile. The soil was black and not sandy. Again, small, ragged children appeared collecting earth to put in the potholes. They held out their hands for money. How I wished we could stop and fill each of those little hands with our coins. I knew it wouldn't solve the problem of poverty. We drove past.

We saw a sign advertising a new hotel "Hotel Kapulana" three kilometres (1.8 miles) north of Gorongosa.

"Maybe that could be a possibility to stay some other time!" Syd said.

He must be joking!

Along the road down a slope there was a sea of yellow buckets. Women pumped at the standpipe to get their water for the day. As we bumped along to Inchope, we stopped to refuel. For the first time we were told there was no diesel. We had a container in the boot with an emergency supply, but perhaps we wouldn't need it.

The goat herder sat on a log as he minded his goats. Just a little further and we came across another service station.

This one had a café. Being few and far between, we could not ignore this opportunity. We stopped. There was a guard with a machine gun. Not what you would expect to see. I got out and approached him to take a photo. He seemed quite friendly and not as menacing as others we had seen. He pointed to my camera and held his hand out and said 1000 meticals. I couldn't believe it. No photo.

The atmosphere in the café was pleasant and the woman understood the word "coffee". No milk, so black coffee it was. This instant coffee was made African style. She stirred that coffee for a full five minutes telling us it must be well blended. "Instant" had lost its meaning.

We set off again and saw the strangest sight. It was a tut-tut (3 wheeled vehicle) with a filled-in cabin and a red cross on the side. It seemed impossible that this small vehicle could be an emergency ambulance. Sirens were piercing the space, confirming its purpose. It must be a limited, local service because further up the road came those potholes.

We drove for hours, looking for appropriate accommodation. Perhaps we missed something on the way up. Nothing and the light begun to fail. We were forced to drive on, for a further two hours. How we managed not to hit something was down to Syd's steel nerves and God's protection.

At last lights appeared. Vilankulo? The dazzling headlights from the oncoming traffic caused us to miss the turnoff. We realised the mistake quickly and turned around. It looked so different in the dark. We turned right now and drove slowly to review the accommodation. We spotted a lodge and before checking in, we drove down to the main street to refuel. No problems.

The lodge was enclosed and seemed safe. It was expensive but we allowed the African to take our money and were shown the room. There was a TV but with no viewing channels. That is extra. There was a shower but no hot water, just a trickle of cold. Hurrah, the bed was comfortable, so we settled down to watch the portable DVD player. We were so tired, the frills of travelling were not necessary. Safety was paramount.

Our journey so far was better than it had been on the way up. Was that because now we knew what to expect? One more day to get back to the border with South Africa before it closed for the night. Would we make it?

## 14. Dreams and Epiphanies

It was a sudden revelation during the night. A reminder from the Lord? We had got our fuel but now we wouldn't have enough money for another tank to get us back to South Africa. We got up at 6 am and dashed down to the ATM in the town and used the international one which we had used on the way up. We were only delayed by twenty minutes from our target. I read a road sign – 520 kilometres to Xai-Xai. That would be our pit stop.

I checked the temperature – the cab was 19.5 degrees and outside 22 degrees. A warm start for the early hour. The lodge provided a good night's sleep. We were both more relaxed. To relieve our boredom as we drove, we made up a song. It was fun and something we had never done together before. It described just how we felt.

> 80 – 60 Mozambeekie
> You must watch your speedy-speedy
> Watch out for the policeman with his gun.
> He is having lots of fun.
> You are traumatised by fining,
> But every cloud has a silver lining.
> Policeman, gun, having fun,
> While he sits out in the sun.

The rhyming was pathetic. The meaning was overdramatized, but we would always remember it.

Why is it that the return journey from a grand adventure – or even just a holiday – seemed twice as long and tedious as the outgoing journey? Was it because there were no new thrills or were our minds already back from the holiday before our bodies reached home? I didn't know but the driving seemed to go on forever.

I had to write down Eugene's directions in reverse so I could check we were on track. I looked out of the window and saw a man selling a monkey. How strange. I thought that had been banned even in Africa.

Another roadblock loomed. Not only tourists this time but those with Moz plates. That was a little reassuring. We were greeted with the usual, "How are you?" quickly followed by "Where are you going?" What difference did it make where we were going?

"Drinkie?"

Syd replied sharply, "No sorry, nothing left."

Surprisingly his refusal was accepted, and the man waved us on.

Easter Monday was a public holiday. We knew that a toll had to be paid at the Rio Save bridge, but we had read that there was no toll on public holidays, so we were surprised to be stopped by an army roadblock as we got to the bridge. This soldier was intimidating. A smileless face demanded money and told Syd to get out of the vehicle.

"There is no toll today. It is a public holiday," Syd said.

"You have to pay," demanded the soldier brandishing his machine gun. That familiar dampness invaded my palms. I tried to look in the mirror without the soldier noticing as I didn't want to incite him. I could just see him and Syd at the side of our vehicle. Their stern faces revealed that neither would back down.

"What have you got in the truck?"

"I want to see your commanding officer," Syd said quite calmly as they walked to the back of the truck.

"Oh, you are very clever, Baba," the soldier replied. He looked into the truck, as Syd pulled a blanket over our tinned food.

My body was wet in the oppressive heat. I could not hear the conversation clearly and hoped Syd was not riling the soldier anymore. Syd was calm but I could see the soldier was agitated. I prayed silently and the soldier walked to the front of the truck. Syd appeared with a tin in his hand and gave it to the soldier who took it and waved us on. Relief flooded over me. For the first time on this trip, I had been uncomfortable with fear. I knew Syd was not a man who would be pushed around. He would stand his ground especially on issues of justice and fairness. But I was painfully aware that we were in Africa, and this soldier had a machine gun and was probably not afraid to use it.

As we approached Maxixe, we spied more up-market resorts. Local people were sitting by the roadside, sharpening knives. They used the edges of other knives to do this. A little further and a service station came into view. A shop and toilets. Amazingly, the toilets were immaculate and working. Disappointingly, the bakery had sold out. No cake for me. At the Maxixe sign, we saw an advertisement for a campsite. I squealed with delight. This was the first one we had ever seen in Mozambique. Also, there was a Kentucky Fried Chicken somewhere. There was a lot of produce being sold along the road – coconuts, melons, mangoes. Little bags of nuts, possibly cashews, hung from a half-dead tree. It looked so funny and reminded me of the nursery rhyme "my little nut tree". Second-hand tyres came into view, and I thanked God we hadn't had a puncture.

A lot of Portuguese style buildings appeared in Inharieme. I wondered if it had special significance in Portuguese Mozambique. Meat was hanging up and obviously for sale. An equivalence of UK health and safety rules did not feature. Goats were riding on the back of a lorry looking uncomfortable. In this area children could be seen playing with toys – a wheel and a stick. Craft stalls also featured, selling seahorses and fish.

At Xai-Xai we stopped at a big supermarket, Saverite, to get something to braai. I waited in the car park, while Syd went inside. Although we had encountered no crime on this trip, I was cautious about leaving our heavy ladened vehicle, unattended. This was a big supermarket more in line with what we were used to. The area seemed densely populated. Children begged for coins, and it seemed to be a common meeting place for customers. I watched as the people greeted each other. A continental influence could be glimpsed as the people kissed each other on both cheeks.

I was glad I had written the instructions in reverse order. It was so much easier to follow. In Macia we stopped again at the Sabores restaurant. Strange isn't it how pleasant it is to visit a restaurant for the second time when your first experience has been good. Something comforting about the familiar.

The route still looked different than what we remembered. Had we gone the wrong way? Was there a rail track crossing the road? I couldn't remember. Was there anyone we could ask? The phrase book was in the back of the truck, not easily accessible. Even if we had it, we probably wouldn't be able to make ourselves understood.

As the dirt track became red earth, and cows wandered across the road in front of us, I was sure we were lost. We had stopped and said to a passerby, "Border, Giroyondo National Park" and were directed along this road. No, that person had definitely misunderstood us. This couldn't be right. Pain cramped my stomach. My throat went dry as the light begun to fade.

Syd cracked a joke, "How did the goats cross the road?"

Not very amused, I answered, "I don't know."

"In front of us."

I didn't split my sides laughing. We were lost. It was getting dark. A quick prayer and an idea came to me. We still had the Moz SIM in the phone. I phoned Eugene. He was there. We were able to ask him a few questions which got us on the right road. As we came to the National Park, we had both forgotten that we had crossed the most amazing bridge when we entered the country. How could I have forgotten it? Later I looked at our photos. There was the bridge! It seemed a million hours away.

We drove to the entry site office to pay for the night, and I was enraged to find out it costs more than a night in the Kruger South Africa; one night's camping and park entry came to R610. I was amazed, but we had no alternative. I remembered to switch the phones off, so they would register a new country after we crossed the border. The African park rangers were very polite and showed us where to pitch our tent. In talking to them, it was obvious that they were Christians. That brought me comfort.

We reached the national park just as darkness fell. We erected the tent and looked for the braai facilities. Sadly, this campsite just wasn't as well equipped as those on the South African side. But the people were friendly. Syd, survivalist supremo, got a sort of fire going and cooked the meat. It tasted decidedly unappetising. We discovered a few scorpions and bugs by the tent, so Syd doomed everything. As I got ready to go to bed, I was gasping for breath and glad we would be back in South Africa tomorrow. As I looked up at the sky, I appreciated one thing. The sky was absolutely clear. There were no cities around. Syd pointed out the Southern Cross to me. For the first time in my life, I could see the Southern Cross and a shooting star. That made it worthwhile. God's glory could be clearly seen in nature. I had an overwhelming feeling of gratitude.

In the morning, I was awakened by the sound of cheerful, female laughter and talking. When I entered the ablution block, it was obvious that the African women were in a group, maybe park rangers, or border officials and, thinking it was only themselves, were stripped half-naked to wash at the basins, oblivious of my presence. As they dried themselves all donned white underwear. The camaraderie between them was obvious and comforting to see. It gave the morning a lift.

On this side of the park, I saw small children walking around which was more evidence that there were no dangerous animals around. The wire strung along the road was of more danger to us and we were careful to avoid it.

An hour and a half later we reached the border and went through the customs and immigration departments. Our fuel was getting low, but the light hadn't yet come on to indicate 'empty'; that was assuming the light was still working. Police and immigration didn't want to check the truck, so we were waved on. We arrived on the South African side at 10.25 am.

We hadn't travelled far when we were stopped. This time it was a park official. His speed gun had registered a speed of 76 kmh in a 50-speed zone. Speeds were limited to protect the animal species. It did seem a little odd that he recorded the speed at 76 kmh. It was even more suspicious when he decided he could reduce the R1000 fine to R250. We paid up. This time the fine was justified. We had been speeding.

Once again, we enjoyed the sight of zebras, herds of giraffe, waterbuck, impala, wildebeest and huge elephants. We bought our lunch at the Bush café at Letaba Rest camp – babootie paninis with vegetables. Very tasty.

We had time to go for one more drive-around. We could only book in for one night due to Easter holiday visitors. There was something to be said for checking the national holidays before you go away. After our experience of Mozambican roads, we appreciated the well-maintained South African roads, even if we had to stop frequently at the Stop-and-Go roadworks.

## 15. Back in South Africa

We started at 6 am on Thursday 20 April 2017. The nearest gate to Letaba was Phalaborwa 51 miles away. Our plan was to take the minor road R71 to Polkewane and then the national road N1. It was not a route we had been on before, but we decided that it would be the quickest way. It seemed as if we had been away for ages but when I worked it out, we had left on the 5$^{th}$ and it was the 20$^{th,}$ making it just 15 days.

> We'll take the high road
> And you take the low road,
> And we'll be in Polkewane before you…

Along the roadside we noticed the change of the quality of goods for sale, reflecting the different economies of Mozambique and South Africa. Tall banana trees alongside the road made good shade for the vendors and mitigated the sweltering heat.

A huge complex "Zion City Maria" dominated the landscape. Tents were pitched everywhere. Was this an Easter special or was it here all the time? The single lane roads multiplied into five-lane carriageways as we continued towards the N1. There were a lot of toll roads; too many to number and the counting out of small change became frustrating.

The early start meant that we reached Kroonstad in the afternoon. Syd was determined to find the campsite that his other sailor friends had told him about. After a little enquiry we found it in the centre of town - not where you would expect to find a campsite. It was really cheap only R130 for two people per night. This time we knew where Kroonpark was to get groceries.

We set up camp and were delighted to find we were the only people on the site. There were also chalets and rooms for hire. We 'braaied' the 'wors' we bought. The facilities were good, but the weather was a little chilly. I wrapped Tina's gift blanket around me and was woken up at 4 am by Syd pulling the covers. It had become very cold. I offered to share my blanket, but the offer was declined. In the morning, I discovered that Syd had misheard me and shivered the whole night quite unnecessarily.

Again, we managed an early start. The showers were beautifully hot – Syd said scalding. The truck keys went missing and, in our search, we discovered they were in the ignition. The cab door was locked so how had this happened? Regardless we tried to retrieve them. We had put a sliding window between the cab and the truck base and by carefully reaching through the window I got them. Just another incident in the lives of the Wellers, or "another fine mess".

The landscape had changed, and the bore hole pumps provided relief from an otherwise boring scene. Eventually we were on the road. Twenty minutes later, we were stopped by the Free State traffic officers. We were relieved it was only a check on driving licences. Within minutes we were off again. I made a mental note to work out how many hours travel we had lost on this trip through police checks. The lorries in this northern part of South Africa had a tradition of beeping their horns as they allowed cars to overtake them. Very weird.

We came to our first Stop-and-Go and we smiled at each other, not complaining after our Moz Road experience. We passed several roads under construction. It was interesting to note the several layers of stones put on before the tarmac. That is why the roads in Moz were so badly worn. The thoroughness of the South African system was missing.

We crossed the Karoo. The fields of golden grass gave way to fields of mielies (sweet corn). The fields of cows were replaced by the occasional ostrich. As we approached Beaufort West the flat land shaped itself into mountains. Bodily, I began to suffer from the intense heat of the past two weeks, as I noticed the rough, dry skin on my feet. I reached for the moisturiser preventing dry and cracked feet and heels.

Syd remembered the days long past, when he and his naval colleagues would do this journey from Johannesburg (or Pretoria) to Cape Town in one day. Then there were no roadworks, not much traffic and you could travel at greater speeds. No lorries made travelling more efficient. As we drove along, we thought of all the pop songs we used to sing as children. We sang through Tommy Steele's 'Little White Bull' and it lightened our tiredness.

At 4 pm we arrived at "Steenbokkies". It was still light so this time we were able to erect the tent properly. We laughed as another camper asked us to help him put his tent up. He had never camped before but had been persuaded by his wife and children to buy a tent for the holidays. He bought the tent that afternoon and hadn't had a chance to try it. It wasn't long before Syd had his tent up as well as ours.

Just before we retired for the night, Syd asked,

"Where is the can of doom?"

"I don't know" I lied.

Unable to keep up the pretence, I admitted I knew where it was. Much to my distaste, we were "doomed" again that night.

# 16. Missions Impossible Completed

It was Saturday 22 April, and we were up at seven. The road was the same one as our outward journey so it held few surprises, but as we passed by the Karoo National Park, we discussed whether it could be a future stopping point if we visited Beaufort West and the surrounding areas again. The sky was clear, and it was sunshine all the way. I was happy to be travelling in South Africa again.

We saw vehicles being towed after an accident and we realised the difference in the driving experience between South Africa and the UK. In the UK we tended to go for pick-up trucks rather than tow vehicles after an accident. Maybe it was something to do with the costs or the greater distances involved in South Africa. Thinking about breakdown, we met someone at "Steenbokkies" who gave us a card for a national breakdown company. Another fear of mine had been addressed. We hadn't managed to join one, but I am increasingly aware that good fortune has smiled on us so far not to have had an accident nor a breakdown. I could say it was the Lord's protection but what about those Christians who do break down and who do have accidents? I wouldn't insult them by making any pretentious claims. I just thanked the Lord and acknowledged His goodness.

This part of the country had rows upon rows of pylons reminding me of the national grid. Often when we travelled, I was unable to connect to electric facilities because of wrong plugs, and the travel books didn't always give you the correct information. We had had to buy a caravan blue converter to use at the rest camps. We needed one for the cooler box and that was a change since last year.

The countryside was changing. There was a large solar farm outside Touwsriver. Certainly, it was an addition since last visit. It changed the landscape but a country with so much sunshine must harness it.

Here there was a plethora of illegal grape and fruit sellers. There was even an official sign which warned us about this misdemeanour. It reminded me of our trading days on the bookstall, and I smiled. All of us want to make some extra money, don't we? For some it was about making a living. This trip had enabled me to reflect on our days in South Africa. How great is our God. He had been good to us.

This road was smooth and there were no bumps or potholes. I appreciated the pleasure of the scenic mountains and the big blue sky. One journey of this year's African holiday was almost complete. Also, our life journey along the grand highway had progressed, and I had been blessed with an abundance of time to ruminate about my life. Our children were now on their own journeys. Each one had developed into a talented human being. Five blessings from God.

God made us into one of his families. Syd and I still journeyed together after 36 years. God had shown me that the difficulties and tragedies of our lives, the blips and bumps in the road, became His opportunities to show us His power and His glory and for me to develop a more Christ-like character. At the beginning of this mammoth trip, I wondered about the ministry and mission of Eugene and Tina and wanted to see for myself, what God had been doing with them. I wanted to support and encourage them. Part of my curiosity though was the burning question of how I would have coped had we been transferred to British Guiana in 2001. The simple answer is that I would have been dead because in 2004, I developed a serious condition, a ruptured bowel, which had I not undergone an emergency operation, I would certainly have died. Would it have been diagnosed correctly in South America? I doubt it. Would I have survived the operation? Maybe not. Although disappointed that we did not go to Guiana, God knew our future so I can say thank you.

A deeper question was about the day-to-day living of missionaries. To some extent, we did experience this at the Bible school. I didn't cope very well and that was only for one week. Could I have handled it for years? If I'm being honest, I would have to say no, I couldn't have done it.

A thought occurred – what exactly is a missionary anyway? My rough definition would be a Christian who is called by God and sent to another culture to spread the good news about Jesus. Eugene and Tina, yes, I would call them missionaries because they were called by God and sent to Mozambique to encourage other Christians to spread the good news about Jesus. As I looked at my own missionary experience in 2001, we were sent by the Council for World Mission, a Christian organisation, from South Africa to share our skills with a partner church in Gloucestershire.

Maybe it didn't feel like a missionary experience because it wasn't. We were sent by an organisation. England was not another culture because we had both been born there. We did tell the people about Jesus, but it was in a pastoral setting. This was no reflection on the Council for World Mission. They did what it said on the tin. They had reviewed their model and goals to reflect missions in the modern world.

Yet **I was** a missionary. The first mission was when God sent us to South Africa to blend two families into one with the love of Jesus. An impossible mission when looked at by the world's eyes. Data on the internet suggested that 60-70% of blended families failed. It was touch-and-go on several occasions but through prayer and reflection the children survived into adulthood, and our marriage survived.

The biggest challenge was to myself to treat all five children fairly, with patience, investing time and effort and required deep self-examination especially when my biological children were in the wrong. This challenge included putting my husband first and working with him as a team for the good of the whole family, not allowing the children to manipulate us, as children of divorced parents often do.

In 1984 I went out to tell people about Jesus and his inclusive love, continuing my journey with different churches and individuals to reach out to a township from a "white" culture, in 1994. We lived in South Africa for 18 years absorbing a totally different culture. I led a project there which involved the soup kitchen, food distribution, clothing sales business, Sunday service, midweek Children's Bible classes, and managed the training of both students and adults on how to engage with a different culture. That was mission impossible 2. This was with the backdrop of the changing society remembering that Nelson Mandela was released from prison on Feb 11, 1990, a time of anxiety and mistrust for the white population. Add into the mix the pressures of being a military wife. Yes, that was a Mission Impossible.

Mission Impossible 3, this trip to Mozambique, was completed by God's grace through my husband Syd's determination, without whom I would have turned back, because of the lack of currency, uncertainty of getting diesel and the horrendous roads. Syd was still on the 'Watch and Wait' programme for prostate cancer, managing his mind and spirit against this awful disease. On the plus side I hope you can read between the lines to see a lifetime of love, and an enduring relationship between Syd and me.

The fear I felt at times on this journey could be compared to the time in 2000 when we were stranded in Harare, Zimbabwe after our passports had been stolen. Then we were in a foreign country with no identification, and we knew no one. We had been on our way to Lusaka, Zambia to explore a call to a Presbyterian church there. We ended up in a black township of 60,000 people and I suspect we were the only white people there. There were political riots at the time. I was shaking involuntarily, unable to eat or drink. Another situation which could be described as a "fine mess".

On this trip of 8231 kilometres (5115 miles), I was able to think about what a missionary is, experience missionary life for myself and realise that an official title and label to the things we do is really not as important as I thought it was.

In our life's journey we do need things like maps to help us on the road, but we also need to trust our God and our Lord Jesus Christ and be guided by the Holy Spirit. On this journey we had gone beyond the map.

# 17. Epilogue

The doctors found a nodule on Syd's prostate in 2021. He completed hormone treatment and radiotherapy on 5 April 2022. He never discussed either the disease nor his treatment. He just got on with it.

As for myself, after several episodes of crippling pain, a severe dent was discovered in the vertebrae of the spine in the neck area. I was offered an operation in 2023 but preferred medication. I do not know whether the cause was the crippling journey we went on but the surgeon said it was probably a factor.

Syd and I celebrated 44 years of marriage recently.

Sad to say, the area where we were in 2017 experienced severe flooding from Storm Idai in 2018 and 2019. Lives were lost. Homes and churches were destroyed. Again in 2026 the southern part of Mozambique, Maputo, was hit by severe storms and flooding. This seriously weakened the roads and infrastructure of the city.

**Acknowledgements**

I acknowledge the help I have received from Christian friends, especially those in the Association of Christian Writers, whose tips have been invaluable in self-publishing this journal. Thank you Stephen Poxon for the foreward and immeasurable tips on the editing process.

I thank Jesus Christ, my Lord, for his strength and power in completing this over a long period of eight years.

My final acknowledgement must go to my husband, Syd, and my wider family, all of whom are an encouragement and support.

# About the Author

Rosalie trained as a primary school teacher as a mature student. During her career, she has taught at all levels and her specialisations include Religious Education, Physical, Social, and Health Education, and English Literature

Combining her teaching skills and a compassionate heart, she developed an outreach project in a South African township, during the years of apartheid. This included a soup kitchen, a feeding scheme, children's services and a clothing distribution self-help scheme.

After retraining at the Bible Institute of South Africa and the University of Cape Town, she was ordained in the Uniting Presbyterian Church of Southern Africa. Her first appointment was as an Evangelist and then Assistant Minister at Fish Hoek Presbyterian church.

In 2001 she was called to a missionary post in Gloucestershire, England, through the Council for World Mission. She is married with five children.

Since retirement, she has focused on writing both poetry and prose. Her published works include several bible study guides, a bereavement journal, inclusion in a devotional year book, and a historical fiction novel.

More information about these can be found on her website, https://rweller3.wixsite.com/rosalieweller .

She is also busy writing a 10-minute reflection and a poem each month for her YouTube channel. She runs a successful writing group, which is affiliated to the Association of Christian Writers (ACW).

If this book has been of help to you, let me know. I can be contacted at

Email: rosalieweller70@gmail.com
Website: https://rweller3.wixsite.com/rosalieweller.com
Instagram rosalie_weller,
Facebook, Rev Rosalie Weller @trustintheLordJesus and onYouTube
https://youtube.com/@ReverendRosalieWeller,

**Other books are available through Amazon**

**Bible Studies and Devotional Books**

**GROW UP** This collection of 16 Bible Studies from the letter to the **Hebrews** is for mature Christians. It tackles the thorny issue of giving up on your faith. At the end of each chapter there are thought-provoking questions to challenge the group. At the end of the book, there are model answers if the study book is being used by an individual to compare their own study answers to the author's. Two original poems by the author are included.

**THE PRISON LETTERS** This collection of 14 Bible Studies is on the letters Paul wrote to the churches while he was in prison in Rome. It includes studies on the letters to the Ephesians, Philippians, Colossians, and the letter to Philemon. Each study is followed by questions which can be used as part of a group bible study. At the end of the book there are model answers which will be particularly valuable for anyone studying as an individual.

**FINDING JESUS** This collection of 12 bible studies is based on the gospel of Luke. It will be particularly useful for those not used to bible study. Each study features a unique part of Jesus' life. At the end of each study there are thought provoking questions for use at group bible studies. At **the** end of the book there are model answers to help any individuals studying on their own.

**LENT AND THE PILGRIM** 15 Bible Studies for the season of Lent and Holy Week. Each study provides commentary and thought-provoking questions on different aspects of Easter. This devotional book will provoke spiritual contemplation.

**IS FAITH ENOUGH? -The letter of James** 12 bible studies which explore the controversial book of James. Both groups and individuals will be challenged by the thought provoking questions at the end of each chapter.

**ADVENT TO EPIPHANY**

43 Seasonal devotional pieces from the first Sunday in Advent to Epiphany Sunday. The underlying theme is that God uses people as His partners in the event of Christ's birth. Not only that but He uses Nature and Pagans. Prayers are included after each reflection.

**Other Books**

Pandemic Peaces
A bereavement journal containing poems, prayers and reflections through the experience of grief as a Christian. Reverend Rosalie's daughter died unexpectedly in 2020.

**Cromwell and Elizabeth – The Beginning**
This is a fiction historical novel centred around the early relationship between Oliver Cromwell and his wife Elizabeth.

Printed in Dunstable, United Kingdom